!NSPIRED TOO
More Performance Coaching Insights from the Front Line

TIM WIGHAM

authorHOUSE®

AuthorHouse™ UK
1663 Liberty Drive
Bloomington, IN 47403 USA
www.authorhouse.co.uk
Phone: 0800.197.4150

© 2018 Tim Wigham. All rights reserved.

No part of this book may be reproduced, stored in a retrieval system, or transmitted by any means without the written permission of the author.

Published by AuthorHouse 02/06/2018

ISBN: 978-1-5462-8661-5 (sc)
ISBN: 978-1-5462-8660-8 (e)

Print information available on the last page.

Any people depicted in stock imagery provided by Thinkstock are models, and such images are being used for illustrative purposes only. Certain stock imagery © Thinkstock.

This book is printed on acid-free paper.

Because of the dynamic nature of the Internet, any web addresses or links contained in this book may have changed since publication and may no longer be valid. The views expressed in this work are solely those of the author and do not necessarily reflect the views of the publisher, and the publisher hereby disclaims any responsibility for them.

Contents

Introduction xi

1. What Is The Value Of Reflection? 1
2. Inspiring Why? 4
3. Which Leading Indicator Is The Best
   Predictor Of Performance Improvement? 7
4. What Is Invisible Lost Time? 11
5. How Do We Make Performance Personal? 15
6. Key Ingredients For High Performance 18
7. How Do We Inspire Through Training? 22
8. Reference Points For Personal Inspiration? 25
9. Workshop 101 28
10. How Do We Stake Our "Claim"? 31
11. Strength And Strategy... 34
12. How Does It Feel To Realise A Dream? 36
13. What Lights Your Fire? 39
14. What Is Illusory Superiority? 42
15. How Do We Close The Deal?..................................45
16. Why Is The Army Navy Day So Inspiring?............ 48
17. Inspired At Leadercast 53
18. Chasing First 56
19. Conditions For Accelerated Collaboration 60
20. Clearing The Fog... 63

21. How Important Is Followership?............................... 66
22. Correlating Lesson Closure With Campaign Performance.. 69
23. What Is Fit For Purpose? 72
24. Path To The Podium 75
25. Lessons From A Proven Entrepreneur 79
26. Best Indicators Of Performance Culture 82
27. Firehouse 51 84
28. Stepping Off The Hamster Wheel 86
29. Forging Identity 88
30. Leading Social Indicators Of A True Team 90
31. How Important Are Reference Points? 93
32. Crossing The Rubicon 95
33. Quotes To Take You Above And Beyond 97
34. Defining Our Approach 99
35. Why Have A Reunion? 102
36. Playing The Sweeper 105
37. How Do We Get The Horse To Drink?..................108
38. How Do We Learn? 111
39. Shackleton Leadership 114
40. Beating Procrastination.. 117
41. Inspiring Poems 120
42. The Value Of Mind Mapping............................... 123
43. Disrupting Inertia..125
44. "Not Broken" To "Needs Fixing" 128
45. The Importance Of Continuity 130
46. Lest We Forget..132
47. Link It All Together...135
48. What Is Your Sentence? 137
49. Challenger To Champion.......................................139

50. Value Perception 142
51. Reel Time 144
52. Best Year Ever 146

About The Author.. 149

For my mother,
Susan Wigham,
the kindest person I know

*Thanks for inspiring me to express myself
and for loving me without condition.*

Introduction

My purpose in life became clear when I had the opportunity to become a performance coach in the heavy industries of the energy sector.

I had loved my time serving the cause of freedom as a Royal Marines Commando, and during my subsequent MBA year I realized I wanted to apply what I had learned about leadership, teamwork, and inspiration, to help other teams be the best they could be.

This evolved as I started a business to help a variety of companies to build strength and strategy, but it was only when I started supporting groups that faced somewhat similar challenges to Marines, that I knew I'd arrived in a place I could add a lot of value.

Diverse teams of men and women, under pressure to deliver results in risky, remote locations, have a problem that needs solving. They require inspiring leadership, structured performance management, and strong teamwork. These are elements I am passionate about and have spent decades researching and striving to understand.

I decided to begin recording my insights for two reasons: first, they help me unpack and explain what I believe and have experienced at the front line helping different project teams; and second, they are a way of sharing my knowledge and giving back to the community to help us all aspire to better team performance.

1
WHAT IS THE VALUE OF REFLECTION?

As one year comes to an end and another makes an entrance, we often find ourselves reflecting on what happened: where we are now and where we want to go.

My epiphany over the last few weeks has been the degree to which I can learn and grow with a genuine and thorough reflection on the recent past.

Looking back at 2016 I discovered a number of breakthroughs and was able to analyse what made the difference compared to previous years. In the case of writing and wellness it boiled down to smaller steps never compromised, rather than big aspirations with insufficient progress-markers to help build momentum.

There were disappointments of course; potential work opportunities unrealized and an imbalance between competing personal priorities. Analysis of these has helped me to refine my approach to business development, and to connect personal goals so that where possible personal priorities can be achieved together.

Interestingly I noticed that I had written down a stretch vision for 2016 back in 2012. I reflected on the list and was surprised that more than half of the items could be ticked off. I've now done the 2020 version.

Very importantly, reflection can and should inspire self-respect, gratitude and recognition. When things are not going our way, we tend to forget some of the positives. Time set aside for reflection ensures that recent achievements are noted and appreciated, it also highlights significant others who have provided love and support to us along the way.

The power of reflection is huge: It is an in-depth retrospect to help us get better. This principle is of course best practice for not just personal but also project improvement. Regular and rigorous performance reviews gather lessons from what went well and not so well. These learnings help teams get better at anything and everything that is sufficiently reviewed. The trouble is that there is no instant "future performance warning" for non-review so we assume it is all right to dismiss the need for regular reflection when in actual-fact staying the same effectively means we are losing ground.

!nspired Too

The value of structured reflection and performance review as a minimum is organised learning, accelerated improvement, appropriate recognition, and in the case of projects, a more cohesive and effective team.

2
INSPIRING WHY?

I've just finished "Start with Why" by Simon Sinek; an inspiring and insightful book which I can thoroughly recommend. In his last chapter, Sinek offers a succinct summary of what distinguishes organizations that start with why.

"We are continually improving at what we do, we come to work to inspire people to do the things that inspire them... If you believe what we believe and you believe that the things we do can help you, then yes, we are better than the competition... Our goal is to find customers who believe what we believe and work together so that we can all succeed, shoulder to shoulder in pursuit of the same goals, not opposite each other in pursuit of a sweeter deal..."

The concept of clients buying why you do what you do, rather than just what you do is a paradigm shift and one which offers a healthy challenge to us all.

"Apple" is used as a strong reference point in Sinek's book due to the company's trail breaking lead in "challenging the status quo" with all that they do. Sky's mantra is "believe in better". The Royal Marines ask if you have the necessary mindset or "state of mind" and believe that 99.9% need not apply. It is the "why" aspiration which inspires interest, commitment, and loyalty from employees and customers alike.

If clients buy why we do what we do, it makes sense to take a moment to be very clear about our "why".

As a performance coach, it certainly helped clarify my "why": I have a personal belief that as individuals and within families and project teams, we are all capable of so much more than our current reality. As a company, we believe that all project teams have strong potential for continuous improvement and innovation; this inspires me and completely aligns with my passion and aspiration.

The longest running client we have had is more of a partner and their belief rhymes perfectly with ours - they believe that their project teams can get better and better and that as a collective, each team has huge potential to be world class. We brought the "how" and "what" expertise at a tactical level to support project leaders in catalyzing the transformation, but the decision to involve us was based on our "why" - that diverse and newly formed project teams have the potential within them to become world class.

Sinek makes the point with which I agree; too many of us get stuck on promoting the "how" and "what" we do, which is important but not necessarily inspiring, certainly not conducive to long term commitment.

Be clear about your "why" and inspire colleagues and clients who believe what you believe. The "how" and "what" will take care of themselves. Thanks Simon.

3

WHICH LEADING INDICATOR IS THE BEST PREDICTOR OF PERFORMANCE IMPROVEMENT?

The correlation between leading and lagging indicators of performance is a fascinating one. Clearly it is also hugely significant given that the lagging indicators are effectively the business results.

I reflected on this recently albeit with a laser focus on the offshore oil and gas industry where I have advised on front line performance improvement for the last 10 years. Lagging indicators tend to be about safety, productivity, efficiency and cost. Leading indicators tend to be about team induction and recognition, safety management participation, efficiency and cost improvement contribution, planning, review, and closing the learning loop.

I trawled the data that we have collected in that time and realised it aligned with my intuition; whilst on all projects there has been clear evidence that improvement and innovation has benefited from a rigorous approach, the difference between the good and great projects has been project leadership adherence to the regular weekly lessons-learned-conference-call.

On projects where there has been performance creep on this fundamental discipline, there has always been performance creep in other key areas as well. Operational reviews have typically slipped and planning rigour has been eroded too. Ultimately, on projects where lip service was paid to the necessity for a weekly lessons-learned-conference-call between the office and the front line, trouble has continued to interfere with progress, and results have been inconsistent.

It is arguably the less tangible benefits of the weekly learning conference call that have the greatest impact and these benefits are therefore most significantly missed when this discipline is dismissed. I am talking here about leadership cohesion, collaboration, camaraderie, mutual respect and a sense of fun - soft elements that are hard to achieve - elements which emerge when stakeholders from different sides of the contract table go through the hard yards together, and become one team with one mission.

An investment in a declared improvement initiative as distinct from assuming that daily business as usual will naturally lead to improvement, is a declaration of intent, it is a signal to the project team that ordinary will not suffice. It is an investment in a project performance legacy. A project less ordinary and more extra-ordinary.

Weekly one hour lessons-learned-conference-calls driven by the project leader convey the following key messages to the team:

1. We do the right thing.
2. We do what we agreed and committed to do.
3. Learning is important for everyone at every level of the operation because we don't know everything; in fact, we are all learning all the time.
4. Going into a repeat operation with a related lesson still open is unprofessional.
5. World class results are driven by a world class team which maintains the highest standards no matter what.

The engine of performance improvement includes planning, review, and closing the learning loop. The way these disciplines are applied may look different from one industry to the next, but they are fundamental in order to grow and learn. They require teamwork and communication, organisation and attention to detail. They require effort.

Our project data conclusively shows that there is a very clear correlation between team adherence to rigorous, professional, weekly lessons-learned-conference-calls, and the slope of the improvement curve for the key measurables of safety, time, and cost.

Capture, discuss, close and implement lessons learned for next time improvement and you will raise the performance bar - guaranteed.

4
WHAT IS INVISIBLE LOST TIME?

Invisible Lost Time (ILT) is the size of the opportunity to improve; it is the gap between current and potential performance. It is sometimes referenced as inefficient lost time. It is time during which progress is still being made on a task but progress that is not as efficient as it should be. It is different from non-productive time during which zero progress is made on the critical path.

Interestingly enough, invisible lost time accounts for a significant amount of project time on most operations, yet it is often ignored or overlooked. On a recent two-well exploration drilling campaign, we focused in on the first well's ILT which represented 25% of the total time taken!

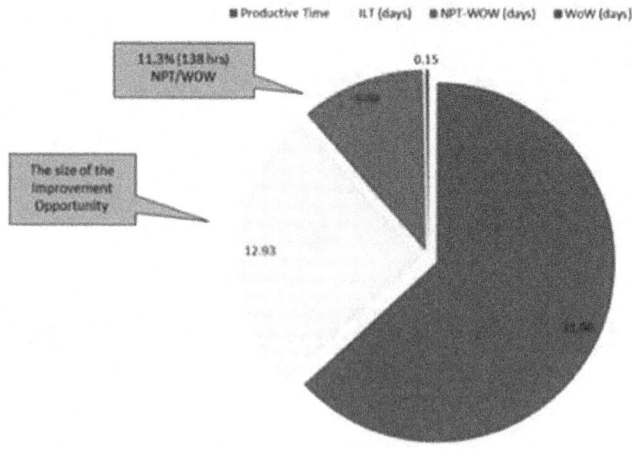

A thorough analysis of this gap between planned and actual time revealed 5 significant areas for team focus on the second well and as a result of that focus, the invisible lost time component reduced from 25% to 10%; equivalent to ~$5 Million of time/cost savings.

There can be a number of possible root causes for ILT, one is the possibility that the planned time was over ambitious in which case the ILT was not really ILT but if this was the case at least the variance and subsequent analysis would have alerted us to the fact that the planned time was unrealistic.

Other common root causes that I have come across over the last ten years include the following:
1. Inadequate pre-job communication and offline preparation.
2. Weak front-line leadership and poor delegation which then allows poor teamwork.

!nspired Too

3. Lack of crew experience and/or disparity in the experience of different crews.
4. Shortage of immediately available mechanical tools to optimise the job and to troubleshoot critical path issues.
5. Indecision during execution.

We have discussed before that projects involve people, processes and appropriate technology or equipment: Reflecting on the common contributors to inefficiency in oil and gas, we are reminded that while it is of course essential to have the right equipment on the rig floor - serviced and ready to deploy, it is even more important that the right supervisors are in place with genuine leadership skills and a thorough understanding of the team and the plan, including contingency options in the event of trouble.

Inexperience requires mentorship and sometimes further training; if these elements are ignored, inexperience can quickly become incompetence and worst case can lead to unnecessary incidents. This would be an example of invisible lost time (ILT) leading to nonproductive time (NPT) due to a lack of attention and correction when the warning signs first emerged.

In summary, invisible lost time is a silent budget killer but worse than that, if left unchecked it can kill morale and threaten personnel safety. Time after time we have seen significant project improvement simply by ensuring that ILT is accurately measured, analysed, discussed and addressed at root cause.

Performance coaches if used, play a fundamental role in conjoining the office based design team with front line operators so that genuine ILT root causes can be established, and salient solutions then embedded into revised programmes.

5
HOW DO WE MAKE PERFORMANCE PERSONAL?

A recent article by someone called Jason Selk reminded me about "Expectancy Theory" which states that whatever you focus on expands.

There is a large body of research around the concept and value of goal setting and visualisation; in my experience, there is no doubt that aiming at a clear target increases the likelihood of hitting it or at least getting closer than if there was no aim or no target at all!

There is a well-known quote about measuring to manage - "if you dont measure, you can't manage". To this end, we establish (daily updated) performance boards and a weekly performance slide on all project installations so that the team's performance against agreed metrics and targets is visible and current. Good news or bad news, everyone is in the loop.

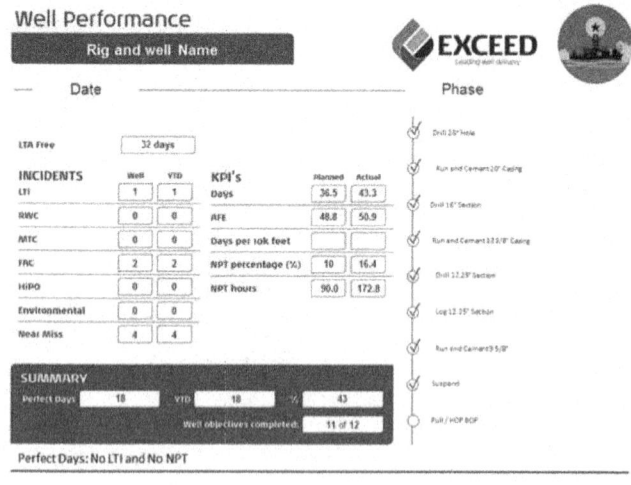

Standard metrics include HSE events, achievement of set objectives, cost, total time and productive time %. Not only are these boards and slides visible but importantly they are also regularly referenced and explained at weekly

!nspired Too

meetings and in monthly newsletters so that all personnel can become familiar with the numbers and charts.

I've been on another project where the performance illustration was even simpler. We had a poster of a barometer and the 100% mark on this represented the stretch target for the financial year. Progress was then updated on a weekly basis such that every member of the team could see the progress relative to target. The barometer was located in a highly visible area of the workplace to ensure focus and awareness.

In order to make performance personal there needs to be a strong connection between leadership and the workforce. Progress needs to be well communicated, clear, and current. Ideally team members need to be able to see how their specific actions contribute to project performance progress.

Bottom line; ensure every stake holder on the project team is given the best possible chance to focus on performance targets and indicators, and we will expand the likelihood of project success.

6
KEY INGREDIENTS FOR HIGH PERFORMANCE

I recently took time out to reflect on the key ingredients for a "continually improving to high performance" project team based on my performance coaching experience over the last ten years in heavy industries on and offshore.

!nspired Too

The following list is hardly a revelation but it is based on real feedback and reinforced observations. Given the performance coaching context, its focus is on people and process rather than equipment and technology.

Leadership - leadership or sponsorship is the beginning and the end of high performance. The style that I believe works best based on my observations is servant leadership as typified by Shackleton or Mandela - humble but resolute; set the example, walk the talk, influence through action, inspire through vision.

Enrolment - stake holders need to be "onboarded". People need to feel respected and heard. This is not a "one off" event, it is an ongoing concern. Team members must feel that they are appreciated and contributing links in the chain. Commitment stems from a sense of inclusion and collective inspiration.

Teamwork - who better than the All Blacks rugby team to exemplify this ingredient. The team needs to be greater than the individuals involved; superstars like Richie McCaw and Dan Carter were not excused from "sweeping the sheds", being humble heroes is part of the legacy and the team integrity. High performing teamwork involves the team members themselves holding each other to an ever-higher standard. The All Black saying goes "leave the jersey in a better state than when you were privileged enough to first pull it on".

Best Practice - this involves constantly benchmarking, analyzing and innovating leading indicators, work processes, tools and behaviours for best results. British cycling is a pertinent example; Dave Brailsford championed the concept of marginal gains in every contributing aspect to overall performance such that tiny tweaks can lead to small wins, larger improvements and ultimately a step change to a podium finish!

Recognition - always recognise and reward stand out effort, contribution, and achievement. A pat on the back with genuine sentiment from a respected leader to a valued team member is more significant than any prize money. The head coach of the Blitz Bokke tweeted after their win at the Wellington Sevens this month "I would go to war for these guys...". Heart felt praise - high performance.

Reflection - average teams don't bother to review past performance in any meaningful way; they tend to carry on doing things the way they've always been done. High performing teams understand that in order to stay ahead of the competition you have to invest in continuous analysis, review, and introspection. It is the whole concept of lessons learned, and learnings implemented.

!nspired Too

In combination, these 6 ingredients are a recipe for campaign success. A compromise on any of them will likely detract from high performance and allow the steady slide to mediocrity.

There are other ingredients and other ways of looking at the concept of high performance but I hope this list provides some food for thought.

7
HOW DO WE INSPIRE THROUGH TRAINING?

Selecting and training performance coaches is a privilege that I will never take for granted. We are always on the lookout for a "few good men" who have the right mindset

!nspired Too

to learn the skillset and embrace the unique challenges associated with an influencing role in high cost, high risk, high ego environments.

The course allows attendees to decide if the performance coach role is for them, while also allowing the course facilitators to gauge who has what it takes to make the transition from a previous position to that of a performance coach.

From a big picture perspective, the aim is to help the prospective coaches experience accelerated team bonding, accelerated learning and inspiring leadership in a safe environment so that they have a reference point for what they will be expected to deliver on behalf of the teams they are fortunate enough to support.

At a personal level, the aim is to introduce the prospective coaches to the tools of performance improvement so that they commence or increase their competence and confidence with skills they may not have had to develop in former roles.

Feedback we have had from previous students regarding what inspires and excites them about the coach training course, points to the learning of new skills such as video editing, or the positive disruption of their frame of reference for something they may have touched on before, such as leadership and presentation skills.

If sessions such as these are instructed by credible experts, and facilitated in a fun, dynamic way, the participants feel they are receiving transferable value and their appetite for some of the more mundane aspects of the course will increase.

Ultimately there needs to be engagement and a sense of personal enhancement for people on a training course to truly achieve enjoyment. Interaction with interesting individuals and informative insights can lead to inspiration and a sense of valuable growth or "time well spent". I personally love facilitating the performance coach training courses because I learn from each and every course member throughout the week: Immersion in the process inspires me every time.

8
REFERENCE POINTS FOR PERSONAL INSPIRATION?

In my final year at school I was the anchor for our house cross country relay team. When I received the baton, I felt the overwhelming weight of responsibility to take the lead and finish strong, instead I mistimed my charge to the front of the field and ultimately failed in my mission, crawled across the finish line, then collapsed unconscious.

I woke up with a drip in each arm and the suggestion that I should not participate in the individual event the following week. Thanks to the sanitorium support, I rehydrated sufficiently for a return to sports in a few days but was initially despondent about my chances in the individual event given the recent fainting incident.

In the end, I felt progressively stronger and more confident as it neared time for the individual run. On the day of the race I got the strategy spot on and found myself in front with 1 km to go. It was then just a case of hanging on, crossing the finish line, and enjoying the taste of victory.

When I look back at this small achievement from my school years, I realise it is a big reference point for how to overcome adversity, find the upside in a downturn, and simply help oneself believe that success can follow disappointment.

After doing 8 years in the Royal Marines, I moved to Cape Town to study an MBA. Being an avid rugby supporter, I was excited to watch the Boks take on the All Blacks that year at Newlands. The evening before the Test Match I bumped into Joost van der Westhuizen by chance. He had always been an inspiring and electric player to watch and I'd listed him along with Nelson Mandela as a legendary South African I would personally love to meet.

Joost went on to play 89 tests for the Boks, he led the team and led the most tries by a Bok for a long time before Bryan Habana eventually overtook him. He was and always will be a hero of South African rugby.

In 2010 Joost was diagnosed with Motor Neuron Disease. Instead of wallowing in self-pity he faced this monster the same way he'd faced down Jonah Lomu in the '95 RWC Final. He championed a foundation to raise money for research to help defeat this terrible disease.

Joost faced many setbacks in his life but he never ever quit. I'm grateful I got to meet him and I find his courage in the face of harrowing adversity to be one of the most inspiring reference points imaginable. He died aged 45 and will be remembered for his indomitable warrior mindset, his unselfish fight for those who may suffer his fate with MND, and his dignity in death.

Reference points for inspiration need to be personal and meaningful. They give us role models, they help bring perspective, and they remind us that what has been done before can be done again.

Don't quit, don't wait, joost do it!

9
WORKSHOP 101

There is always value in requesting feedback from the client sponsor of a workshop. In this case we facilitated a planning and risk assessment session in Aberdeen to ensure no stone is left unturned in readiness for the client's forthcoming abandonment campaign.

!nspired Too

The feedback reinforced many of the known benefits of outsourcing workshop preparation, facilitation, and post workshop transcription to a team of professionals who specialize in accelerated project performance improvement.

1. Event organisation: the client should be protected from any time-consuming administration given their busy operational focus.

2. Stake holder representation: significant effort should be made to ensure that all specialists are in attendance and that front-line personnel are there in number.

3. Time value maximization: set the best possible agenda to achieve the workshop objectives and then ensure that a fine balance is maintained between delivering to deadlines and being flexible when certain issues need to be further explored, often in deliberate focus groups.

4. Accurate record keeping: clearly it is crucial that issues, actions, risks and programme improvements are accurately and comprehensively spelled out and subsequently captured for further examination and resolution.

5. Setting the standard: the professionalism, team interaction and intellectual rigour evidenced at the workshop establish the expectation for the project, in other words - start as you mean to go on.

Of course, as with all things there will be room for improvement after every workshop. In this case we identified an opportunity to be smarter in our organisation of the groups for the discussion sessions, and in our prioritization of key issues requiring special focus teams. A wash-up of the first major project evolution also sets the right precedent for all operations to follow.

Finally, optional initiatives such as a comprehensive project workshop, require strong and visionary leadership in order to take place at all; another reminder that high performance starts with exceptional project leadership.

10

HOW DO WE STAKE OUR "CLAIM"?

In 1990 I recovered from a disappointing collapse during School Cross Country relays to then win the individual Cross Country race the following week.

In 2000 I planned and led part of the Commando fire plan in defence of Freetown, Sierra Leone such that peace could be restored in the West African country.

In 2010 I watched with significant relief as my first daughter was born by caesarean section after complications during natural birth.

In preparation for a talk on Creative Leadership at Robert Gordon University I recently reflected on these as 3 meaningful life experiences which required different types of leadership in each case.

In the first example, I needed to lead myself from doubt to determination, in the second I needed to coordinate a large team effort amid confusion and chaos, in the third I needed to stand back and trust the experts whilst providing whatever moral support I could to my wife!

On reflection, I realised in each example that I felt very alive, inspired, and motivated. This led me to consider the acronym CLAIM:

Creative – Leadership - happens when we are - Alive – Inspired – Motivated

I reflected on my specific reference points again and identified certain conditions which support my personal CLAIM.

1. Healthy competition in a field I am passionate about.

2. Stepping outside my comfort zone while doing something meaningful for others.

3. Successful collaboration during complex challenges involving a diverse team.

!nspired Too

Understanding what conditions enable our Creative Leadership can be a real competitive advantage and indeed feeling Alive, Inspired and Motivated is surely a worthwhile place to find.

Stake your CLAIM and enjoy more accessible Creative Leadership!

11
STRENGTH AND STRATEGY

I recently had the privilege of facilitating a management team breakaway for a company in the Nuclear Sector. The team was interested in a transferable improvement approach from other industries including the military and oil and gas.

We shaped an agenda which focused on building a stronger team on day one and a stronger forward strategy on day two. As with all good workshops, we kept it dynamic, interactive, and always slightly outside the comfort zone such that true learning and "outside the box thinking" was essential.

Using the Gallup Strengths Finder reports for each team member's top 5 strengths, we created the space and time for each person to explain their respective strengths and indeed whether they felt their current role made the most of these strengths. Group feedback to each individual promoted further awareness and ensured that constructive dialogue evolved regarding business value and using the right people for the right tasks based on their strengths profile.

Envisaging a desired future which addresses the rapidly changing market landscape required creativity and clarity, especially when the teams only had 3 hours to convert their ideas into a 3-minute movie. Engagement was excellent and the exercise served as a bridge between strength and strategy.

Day 2 dove further into the steps required to get from current reality to desired future but also drew on learnings from performance improvement in the oil and gas industry which has faced similar challenges in terms of cost efficiency and risk management. Teams worked hard to identify clear aspirations and concrete actions to mitigate market forces, and finally each individual recorded their measurable commitment to the team for 2017.

A strong strategy is key for survival and a strong team knows the strengths of its members. Focusing on what we do have and what we can do has a compound effect on confidence and resilience in the face of uncertainty and change. I learned a lot facilitating the process; witnessing renewed team cohesion was as humbling as ever.

12

HOW DOES IT FEEL TO REALISE A DREAM?

I have dreamed of becoming an author for a long time, perhaps for over ten years.

Last week I held the first copy of my first real book and tried to savour the moment - to really appreciate the tangible and visible result of disciplined endeavour.

There has been no shortage of inspiration or subject matter; the challenge has been simply to knuckle down and get the first book done! Working with extremely diverse people in a variety of different places whilst under pressure to help pull teams together and achieve high performance, has inevitably provided innumerable examples of stand-out leadership, teamwork, and innovation.

To all those I have had the privilege to serve at the front line as a school leader, a marine, a facilitator, a project manager and a performance coach, I owe you a debt of gratitude. It is your effort, your impact, and your resourcefulness that has inspired my belief that we are all capable of so much more. I am passionate about accelerated team unity and team results especially against the odds in a challenging, dynamic environment.

One of my goals for 2016 was to publish a LinkedIn post every week of the year. My original intent was to promote to the oil-and-gas industry how performance coaching helps project teams, while providing nuggets of information about accelerated improvement, inspiring leadership, and innovative collaboration to my LinkedIn network in general.

The reality is that I discovered my calling. I found that as the year progressed, I had more ideas, not fewer, about what subject matter to explore next. I found that the words just flowed onto the pages and that I looked forward to publishing something new each week. It was not a chore; it was an indulgence! More importantly, my articles seemed to generate discussion and attract a positive response. This made me realize that there was a demand for what I enjoy offering the community - performance coaching insights from the front line.

My first book is the first instalment of fifty-two insights, bound together for reference, and all inspired by real experience, observation, and intuition as a front line performance coach.

For interested leaders and coaches, the book is available on Amazon, iTunes and Author House and can be ordered as an e-book or in soft cover.

Be !nspired and enjoy the insights, thanks for your support.

13
WHAT LIGHTS YOUR FIRE?

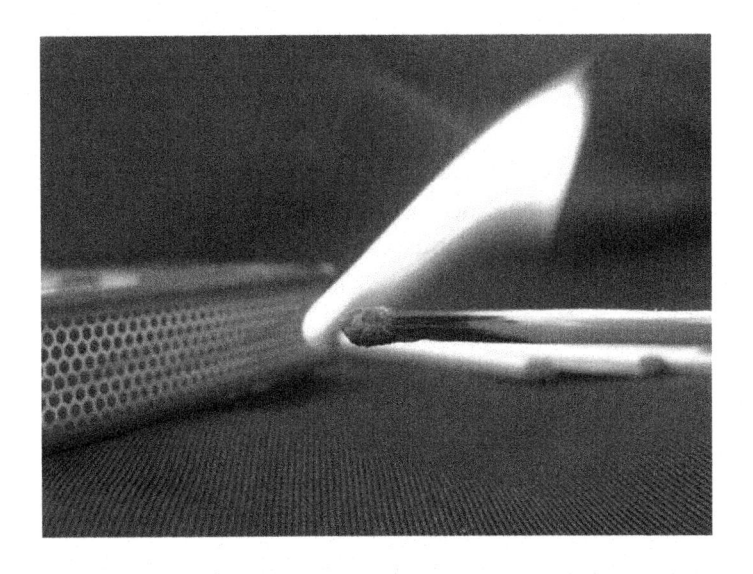

An excellent quote recently caught my eye; "managers light a fire under you, leaders light a fire within you"...

I have been listening to a Les Brown Audio Book compilation over the last few weeks. He emphasises the importance of manifesting your dreams. He inspires, motivates, and persuades using personal anecdotes and professional learning to emphasise the following points:

1. It's possible (to achieve your dream).
2. It's necessary (to pursue your dream).
3. It's worth it (in the end, no matter the sacrifice, as long as you are being true to yourself and doing what you are passionate about even if it is initially tough).

To create a spark, we need friction and traction - we need energy and synergy. When I was looking at my options beyond military life, I identified the MBA as an excellent catalyst for my professional journey, a way of harnessing my transferable skills and channelling them to create value in the commercial world. It was only when I took action to actually visit the business school in Cape Town and invest in the application process that my fire was fuelled and there was no turning back.

Beyond business school, one of the tools which helped me crystallise my thinking about why and how I wanted to do what I wanted to do, was the book "What colour is your parachute" by Richard Nelson Bolles. This book takes a structured approach to helping you figure out your future, and emphasises the importance of pursuing what you are considered an expert at as well as what you really enjoy doing; often those two answers coincide.

In "Good to Great" by Jim Collins, he talks about the Hedgehog Concept: Three overlapping circles: What lights your fire ("passion")? What could you be best in the world at ("best at")? What makes you money ("economic engine")?

!nspired Too

Common to most respected guidance on the matter of creating value and achieving success is the key question of what are you passionate about, what do you enjoy doing, what lights your fire? If you can honestly figure that out and find work which allows you to express your passion, you are in the top 15% of world workers according to recent Gallup surveys.

It is never too late to confirm what lights your fire but don't leave it too late to actually ignite the flame.

14
WHAT IS ILLUSORY SUPERIORITY?

Wikipedia describes illusory superiority as a cognitive bias whereby individuals overestimate their own qualities and abilities, relative to others. This is evident in a variety of areas including intelligence, performance on tasks or tests, and the possession of desirable characteristics or personality traits.

!nspired Too

The Dunning-Kruger effect is interesting. It reminds me of the well-worn comment: "He knows just enough to be dangerous!" It also forces me to reflect on its relevance to my own experience.

A clear example for me is my experience with the sport of fitness (CrossFit); as a relatively fit individual with a fitness award from Royal Marines training, and Royal Navy representation in track and rugby, I entered my first CrossFit Open with a high degree of confidence after only a short period of experience with the sport. I was rapidly humbled by the intensity and difficulty of the challenges and there is no doubt my confidence crashed as I realised the extent of my weaknesses!

After 5 years of improving at CrossFit (while juggling a busy career and family), I would say my confidence is now on the rise. I am far from expert level but I do now compete in the Open and other Masters Competitions with increasing confidence based on commitment, coaching, and continuity.

I am currently listening to the audio book "The Greatest" by Matthew Syed. He touches on the concept of illusory superiority in relation to sportsmen and women, and how in many cases these individuals have rebelled or retired after being dropped from a team or criticised in one way or another. Rather than using a defeat or demotion as motivation to come back stronger, "egomaniacs and prima donnas" tend to over react and burn the bridge.

In the pursuit of high performance, individuals with this cognitive bias can be a major handicap for any team; if they are project leaders or front-line supervisors, they can be dangerous.

In the movie "Deepwater Horizon" the depiction of some project leaders (rightly or wrongly) suggests strong arrogance and ignorance which aligns to this topic. Despite appeals from team members, and emerging information which should have caused alarm and caution, leaders stubbornly pressed on towards a tragic disaster.

The Dunning-Kruger effect has applied to a few leadership teams I've been privileged to performance-culture-assess in the past. Their pre-project "self-assessment" confidence has been somewhat higher than the assessment of their front-line team. During execution, their confidence has been eroded as trouble occurs, but once the entire team pulls together and works as one, good-to-great performance is eventually attained, and earned confidence is restored.

For me, the useful reminder after a quick study of these concepts, is that on complex projects where there is high risk, high cost, and a high chance that no one is an expert at everything, it makes sense to ensure that the diverse strengths within the team are harnessed and optimised.

On most projects with which I have been involved as a performance coach, the key front line leaders recognise this point and wholeheartedly support a team improvement initiative to ensure that no one believes they are above the potential for human error. "Keeping it real" tends to prevent delusions of grandeur and top leaders and teams tend to do exactly that.

As SAP CEO Bill McDermott put it: "Stay hungry, stay humble".

15

HOW DO WE CLOSE THE DEAL?

I reflected recently on a deal I was involved in closing. As with many successful achievements, it was a team event so this is not a focus on what I did to close the deal but rather a list of the more significant check points that were carefully navigated en-route to a positive result.

Keep your ear to the ground - I am a great believer that in general life as much as in business, a huge number of opportunities come our way but we often struggle to capitalise on them for various reasons. My reminded learning is that if we keep our ear to the ground, we will be amazed at the number of opportunities that present themselves albeit often in subtle ways.

Seize the opportunity - "Time waits for no man" goes the saying. It is vital to grab the chance when it is presented in order to either establish momentum, or discover that for one reason or another this is not going to evolve into a real deal. Establish what needs to be done and do it. As Eminem rapped in "Lose Yourself", "You own it".

Connect with decision makers - Many an opportunity has melted away like snow in the morning sun, because the service provider is not speaking to the prospect decision maker. It is essential to politely but persistently probe for information and dialogue with the right potential project sponsors.

Understand the process - There are often nuances that distinguish one bidding process from another and these clearly need to be scrutinised multiple times for confidence and competitiveness. Fundamentally, we "have to be in it to win it". Stay ahead of the game through a clear understanding of the steps involved in getting across the finish line.

Confirm the requirement aligns with your core offer - Let us keep this simple; there is a huge opportunity cost involved in chasing work which requires something different to what we offer at a world class standard. While there are exceptions, generally the more equal the prospect

!nspired Too

requirement is to our well endorsed offer, the more chance there is of success. Ideally it will be a perfect match.

Follow instructions to the letter - Many qualified bidders fail to answer the questions asked and/or fail to submit their response on time. We need to remember that there is no second chance at a first impression. Ensure a bid is received and ensure nothing is missing from what was sent, then clarify when a contract award decision is likely to be made.

Be prepared - I am currently reading a book called "So good they can't ignore you" by Cal Newport; in summary, the book promotes the importance of proven and market leading skills and testimonials such that your brand and offer cannot be ignored because it is so compelling. This is not about arrogance but about confidence based on ceaseless toil and tenacity. Malcolm Gladwell talked about accumulative advantage in his book "Outliers - the story of success". If our service is a never-ending journey to become better and to add more value, and if this is recognised by the target market, we can be cautiously optimistic that we will win the work for which we are bidding.

Closing the deal basically means getting what we deserve. I am reminded of the well-known quote: "Success happens when preparation meets opportunity". Be prepared and keep your ear to the ground!

16

WHY IS THE ARMY NAVY DAY SO INSPIRING?

A former Royal Navy rugby player and friend of mine - Chris - died suddenly last year. He was only 52. His loss was a huge tragedy and he was mourned by many who knew him for the stand out gentleman that he was. One of the causes he was passionate about was the plight of service personnel with PTSD and he'd been instrumental in the promotion of "The Mountain Way", which helps veterans with this condition.

Another friend of mine who also served and played with Chris is Kurt - an exceptional former Navy rugby player and former marine. Kurt contacted me a few weeks ago to explain that Chris had bequeathed some money in his will to be used by friends of his to celebrate his life at his most loved event - the Army Navy game. It was an honour and privilege to be invited.

It was the 100th British Army v Royal Navy match at Twickenham which in itself was special. It was also a sold-out stadium (85,000 people) which is incredible when you remember that in the '90s a crowd of 25,000 for this match was a lot.

I met up with Kurt ahead of the Vets game in the morning and we picked up the conversation where we'd left off when I last saw him 20 years ago! I reflected throughout the day on a number of truly inspiring elements of the experience.

1. The Camaraderie

The British Armed Forces is one big family; this event certainly feels like one BIG reunion. Given the extent of military service and sacrifice particularly over the last 15 years since "9/11", it is a particularly poignant reunion. Many lives have been lost in combat, many alive have scars on minds and bodies. For veterans of the brutal campaigns in Afghanistan and Iraq, as well as the ongoing war on terror, the Army Navy game has become one of the major annual opportunities to reunite with comrades, and to celebrate life and liberty.

I bumped into dozens of old friends with whom I served in the 90's. We caught up and reminisced until we bumped into another old friend and so it went on...

The network established while serving is equally key for business development, this reunion contributes to professional growth; my discussions with Kurt bore this out.

2. The Contest

Twickenham is a modern-day colosseum befitting the gladiators who grace her glorious green pitch.

85,000 spectators were treated to a magnificent contest involving 49 points in all; some superb tries, some bone-shaking tackles, and some breath-taking runs which brought the crowd to their feet and raised the roof with their roars.

I was very impressed by the quality of rugby on display especially when you consider that these are serving personnel in a stretched British military: Achieving consistency and continuity in this context must be a significant challenge.

There is also an accepted truth which is that the Army will generally start as favourites but there is always the chance of an upset. The Navy statistically wins only once every six years nowadays but as a former marine and player myself, I believed the Navy could do it even when there was only one minute left on the clock!

In the end, the Army won 29-20 but the Navy played their hearts out - I was proud of them. The contest was hard fought and played with guts, determination, dignity and respect. The Army had some real x-factor players with lightning speed, they also converted their opportunities into points every time.

3. The Commitment

Player commitment was there for all to see but what about spectator commitment? Armed Forces serving personnel and veterans had travelled from near and far to make the occasion. There were also thousands of civilian rugby fans and British patriots.

Beyond that there was real commitment in terms of dress! Fancy dress. Whether a Corps coloured suit or impressive, authentic "drag" - supporters had gone to town.

Many conversations I joined were focused on finding ways to help those suffering from mental stress and PTSD. There was a real commitment to raise awareness and funds to mitigate and manage what has become a significant problem by many accounts. What was most humbling was that in some cases, the people collaborating to create a charity or join forces in the fight against PTSD, were struggling themselves but their focus was on helping those even less fortunate.

Prince Harry presided over the match as guest of honour and indeed his Invictus initiative was the nominated charity for this year's event. This seemed entirely appropriate and continues the theme of "help for heroes". He was surrounded by some of the wounded Paralympic athletes who have inspired us all at the Invictus Games.

In conclusion, the day was a perfect match for Chris whose life we celebrated. He was an incredible comrade to hundreds of people during his career. He played at Twickenham in the Army Navy game and loved the contest and the challenge. His commitment on the field as a Number 9 was a prelude to his subsequent commitment to values-driven leadership development, and his passion for the "Mountain Way".

I left London inspired and humbled. So many heroes in one day. And what an amazing gesture from this servant leader - to bequeath a pot of money in his will for good friends who shared his passion for the Army Navy game, to enjoy the occasion on his behalf. Goose bumps every time...

17
INSPIRED AT LEADERCAST

There were some exceptional speakers at Leadercast Aberdeen this year; leaders who have "been there" and "bought the T-shirt". Jennifer Young, Ray Riddoch and Bob Keiller really embraced their opportunity to influence other leaders at the AECC.

They each had pearls of wisdom to impart regarding the theme "Lead with Purpose"; I've selected the 3 most illuminating to me based on intuition and experience.
1. Don't try and be someone you are not.
2. Adjust your sails in bad wind to keep sailing.
3. Build trust in accordance with the *trust-equation* from "The Trusted Advisor" (look it up!).

Gavin Oattes was an energetic host and reminded us all of the incredible lessons we can learn from children. Looking at the world through the eyes of a 5-year-old, we realise... a) impossible is nothing, b) excitement is contagious, c) truth sets us free.

We then linked in to the feed from the States and enjoyed more paradigm shifting insights: My epiphany struck during the presentation from Don Miller.

Don's message served me as a Company Director and a Performance Coach:

Clients are not interested in your story, they are interested in their story

If you confuse you'll lose.

Be the guide in "the story".

The ubiquitous story involves a character (client), with a problem (issue that needs solving), who meets a guide (credible, reliable, valuable accountability partner), who provides a plan (service/product) and calls (inspires) the character (client) to action - resulting in success (or failure if things go wrong).

Exceptional leaders are guides who listen to the team, are crystal clear with their plan, and inspire action to achieve success: JFK said, "we'll put a man on the moon", Trump

!nspired Too

said "make America great again"; no matter our politics, these US Presidents accurately read the prevailing story and galvanised the audience. As a result, they won the vote.

I was inspired throughout the day and genuinely learned new tools and skills for more effective leadership in personal and business development, and in business delivery.

18
CHASING FIRST

Three sports I love are Rugby, Athletics, and Crossfit. Because I love them, I watch them and of course I therefore join the league of fans who get inspired by the best. We have recently been treated to movies by three of the best ever; McCaw stars in "Chasing Great", Farah in "No Easy Mile" and Froning in "The Fittest Man in History". There are

!nspired Too

also books about these sportsmen so we can enjoy watching their achievements whilst also studying what makes them tick, what makes a champion, and what drives them on. For athletics, I have chosen Farah because he is a distance runner and there is a common thread of endurance with these three athletes. Bolt is arguably a more successful track athlete than Farah, and of course a legend in his own right!

The obvious striking similarity across all stories is Failure. Each of these legends failed significantly en route to greatness. Richie McCaw led the All Blacks to spectacular failure against France in the 2007 Rugby World Cup Quarter Final in Cardiff. Mo Farah, was well beaten in the Beijing Olympics 2008. Rich Froning famously failed to climb the rope at the 2010 CrossFit Games. These failures came when the athletes expected to win. In each case what happened next was most significant; these guys resolved to learn from their failure, and to get it right next time out.

The key habit I noted from Richie McCaw in "Chasing Great" was his meticulous planning for every game, but specifically the way he wrote "start again" on every new page. Even when he was being hailed as the greatest ever, he had the groundedness to go back to the drawing board. This is the very paradox of greatness - get the basics right. Being part of the All Blacks, he was also moulded by their culture of service to the legacy, respect for those who went before, "sweep the sheds" for the team.

The key habit I noted from Mo Farah was his application to training; relentless mileage on all terrain, always running, always training, often on his own - the "loneliness of the long-distance runner". He had benchmarked the best - the Kenyans. He had lost to them enough times to know that he needed to match and outsmart the best in order to reach the top. This is exactly what he did which led to supreme confidence at the start-line, and a now trademarked "phenomenal final lap".

The key habit I noted from Rich Froning was his Christian faith. After failing to win the 2010 CrossFit Games he reflected on his mindset which was in his opinion too focused on himself rather than on glorifying God. To this end, he committed to putting God first and this is literally engraved in his approach with the application of a permanent tattoo - "Galations 6:14" ["May I never boast except in the cross of our Lord Jesus Christ, through which the world has been crucified to me, and I to the world"].

These athletes are among the best ever in their respective sports. McCaw has won two Rugby World Cups as Captain, Farah has won the 5,000m and 10,000m at two consecutive Olympic Games, Froning won four consecutive CrossFit Games titles as an individual and then immediately led a team to two team titles.

Key takeaways from my perspective...

1. These guys are just inspiring and their movies are well worth having in your Inspiration Library!
2. Set audacious goals but be prepared to Fail on your way to being the best you can be.
3. Stay grounded, stay humble, work hard, earn the right to be confident at the start line.
4. Mental toughness is the competitive edge, these three athletes all invested significant time in building a strong champion mindset; they believe they will win even when everyone watching is doubting them.
5. Have Faith!

!nspired Too

We can all do a lot worse than striving for the Champion Mindset demonstrated by these three role models. These ordinary men have become heroes but they all came from humble beginnings. They also remain firmly connected to their roots and their family values.

If we strive to unleash our potential, no doubt we will surprise and inspire ourselves.

19
CONDITIONS FOR ACCELERATED COLLABORATION

We are privileged to be supporting a number of decommissioning campaigns in the North Sea. For these clients, the amount of learning and the number of wells to be abandoned, justifies the decision to invest in expertise to accelerate collaboration.

In readiness for a significant AWOP last week to kick off one of these campaigns, I reflected on a key aspect of my role as a performance coach: As with many sports coaches, we need to create the right conditions for optimal team induction, integration, interface, and improvement. This applies during readiness for execution, during the campaign itself, and as part of the execution review.

It is generally accepted that all leaders and teams are capable of so much more than is often achieved. The difference between good and excellent often comes down to the extra attention to detail, the extra lessons recorded, the extra mile. The reality is that it also helps to have an extra hand but more particularly, a hand with the skills and accountability to help project leaders build a strong team, and to implement a proven process to enhance detailed planning, communication, learning and recognition.

When referencing experienced oilfield personnel, we often hear the comment, "he's probably forgotten more than you'll ever know!" and that is exactly the problem we help to mitigate in the quest for team excellence. By creating the conditions for programme interrogation and group interaction up front, and by capturing all knowledge throughout the campaign, we ensure that we no longer "forget", and if we've done something once, we "know". We have to tap into the decades of experience that certain oilfield veterans bring to the table; it would be a crying shame not to access that accumulated learning.

Abandoning the Well on Paper (AWOP) actually ensures we draw on the assembled expertise to tap into everyone's knowledge and to do what we can to get operations right first time. Thereafter, we strive to "repeat our successes and learn from our mistakes".

Setting the scene and creating the conditions for excellence is a subtle but significant art. The right planning environment, the right agenda, the right messages and the right material, all add up to getting it right when it counts. These contributing factors, leading indicators and marginal gains, are the difference, the competitive advantage.

Sir Alex Ferguson said this about his success at Manchester United: "The key to it all is preparation and the application of that preparation over time... once you bid farewell to discipline you say goodbye to success". He knew a thing or two about creating the conditions for accelerated collaboration and high performance.

Fast learning and strong teamwork is a business imperative in the current cost climate of decommissioning. One of our clients has now completed their first abandonment under budget thanks to disciplined preparation, strong teamwork, and fast learning. In addition, 100+ lessons were captured and of those, 60+ % are now closed to reduce more cost on the next repeat. The end justifies the means.

20

CLEARING THE FOG

I was recently afflicted by conjunctivitis although initially I just thought I had an irritated eye. As the days wore on, my vision became more and more blurred until I felt like I was operating in thick fog. The blur soon affected both eyes and no amount of blinking or "windscreen wiping" with normal eye drops would clear the view!

I hoped that the fogginess would naturally recede after several days but sadly not. I finally took myself to the pharmacy where the condition was diagnosed and antibiotic drops prescribed. The first of these drops in each eye almost immediately cleared the fog along with the associated discomfort. I felt like a new person!

During the evenings that I was enduring the blurred vision, I pondered several analogies and ironies which I wanted to record and share for reference.

The Fog of War - I had friends involved in the Iraq War 2003 and I remember hearing at one stage that a few were unaccounted for - feared dead. It subsequently transpired that they were safe and alive. When I asked about the confusion my colleague answered, "lack of information, the fog of war". In this case a lack of clarity can be caused by insufficient intelligence, insufficient visibility and poor communication.

Blurred Lines - In my experience domestic and professional conflict is often caused when it is unclear who is in charge, who is in command and who needs to follow and support. Often issues are identified but no-one is assigned ownership to address, close, and implement for resolution and improvement.

Crystal Clear - There are many metaphors we use - "the penny dropped", "the light went on", "eureka moment" and we all know the satisfaction of that sudden clarity after a period of confusion. Stand-out leaders and organisations master this crystal clarity and tend to leave less impressive peers meandering in the fog.

My brief but real frustration with restricted eye sight reminded me how much we take for granted in terms of our basic health and wellness. Is there a more important investment than long term health?

The distinction between foggy and clear also served as a great reference for leadership and performance. Understanding what it takes to mitigate the fog of war, to avoid blurred lines, and to inspire with crystal clarity, is surely a vision worth striving for.

21

HOW IMPORTANT IS FOLLOWERSHIP?

The concept of followership has attracted growing interest in recent times and it is certainly a favourite topic of mine. Perhaps it is because I went to a traditional boarding school, or perhaps it was my time in the military. Either way, I feel that good followership is as important as good leadership. In fact, I'll go a step further and say good followership is good leadership.

There are a few well known quotes which remind us that it is not helpful to have too many people trying to be in charge. "Too many Chiefs and not enough Indians" is one such quote and we can all relate to scenarios where there is conflict in the crowded head office, and a shortage of competent, motivated, productive followers at the front line.

While we quite rightly place significant emphasis on appropriate leadership, we often forget that the very concept of leadership requires followership: "Leadership is a process of influence between a leader and those who are followers" - a quote I have come across before.

When I was a Young Officer in Commando Training we would deploy on field exercises and assume leadership and followership roles based on a schedule of command appointments. In an extreme scenario, one minute you could be in charge of 100 people, the next minute you could be following orders, in charge of no one but yourself and your kit. If leaders did not lead and followers did not follow, the machine broke down - it was and is a mutually beneficial symbiotic relationship in its clearest form.

While the commercial world is not as regimented as the Marines, many organisations could still benefit from a clearer leader/follower paradigm. An example of what I mean could be picking the right forum to challenge a business leader's decision. It is not a case of following blindly but appointed leaders who have reached their position fairly, deserve and require followers to unite behind the agreed mission in order to collectively succeed. If followers have issues with the leader, it is important that challenges are conveyed at the right time, in the right place.

In a family setting we can all relate to the confusion and frustration that can manifest when it is unclear who is leading and when "followers" are uncooperative. What tends to work well is when one parent accepts the situational importance of following the other's lead, and setting an example to the children regarding good followership.

Followership is defined as the ability or willingness to follow a leader. We often discuss how a leader inspires followers, however, we should also acknowledge the courage and leadership it takes to selflessly follow in order to help the team be the best it can be.

22

CORRELATING LESSON CLOSURE WITH CAMPAIGN PERFORMANCE

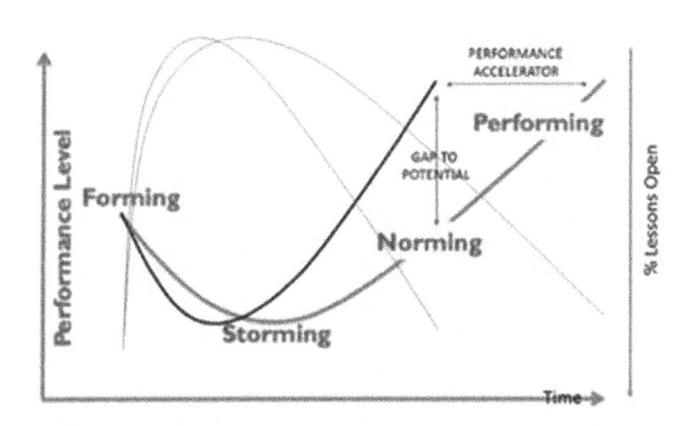

Last year I wrote an article about performance improvement acceleration and how the influence of a focused performance improvement initiative can accelerate the Tuckman team growth curve.

Tim Wigham

During my research and analysis of 20+ oil and gas projects which I've supported as a performance guide since 2007, I have identified a correlation between the timeous and rigorous closure of lessons learned, and the achievement of success as measured by standard lagging indicators.

The most important leading indicator of performance improvement from my analysis is the regular lessons-learned close out call as discussed before. This "call" requires the right people on a conference call every week and assumes that the front-line team has a resource dedicated to diligently and accurately "hunter-gathering" all significant learnings from every day and every phase, reported in quality-checked after-action reviews, and entered into a lessons learned (LL) register which is filtered for focused discussion.

This discipline ensures that the lesson closing imperative is given the highest priority and it drives down the percentage of lessons open especially early on when there is a tidal wave of learning from the front line as the project plan is executed in anger.

The LL call is a perfect combination and representation of the hard and soft skills necessary to optimise performance: The team needs to collaborate and communicate whilst also drawing on diverse technical expertise to trouble-shoot, overcome, and consider different process and equipment solutions to emerging problems.

It got me thinking about a sporting example currently underway; the British and Irish Lions rugby tour of New Zealand. The chart above will definitely apply as the squad goes through the "storming" phase of Tuckman's curve in a desperate bid to arrive at high performance before the three Test Matches against the All Blacks. According to my research and experience with teams in the military and heavy industry, the degree to which the Lions leadership team is able to capture and efficiently address every available lesson, the earlier they will be able to answer questions and realise their true potential.

Like any world class open-side fetcher scavenging for the rugby ball, a project team needs a resource whose primary purpose is to hunt for lessons and then secure them in such a way that the team can consider the next move and keep going forward to win the game.

I truly believe all leaders and teams are capable of more than they have achieved to date. The challenge is how to close the gap to potential and accelerate performance improvement? One guaranteed contributor based on thorough research is a lesson predator and then a pride of leaders willing to sacrifice time each week to strengthen identified weaknesses in order to hit high performance and win the campaign.

23
WHAT IS FIT FOR PURPOSE?

We've all heard the expression "square peg, round hole" and many of us can immediately apply that metaphor to a work or life experience whereby someone (perhaps even ourselves) has been given a role or responsibility which is clearly unsuitable and sadly in many cases, has had a disappointing end.

It ties into a point I made in a previous article regarding the quote about judging a fish by its ability to climb a tree i.e. optimise individual strengths rather than judging weaknesses. Get the right people in the right positions and we have a chance. Align personal purpose to organisational purpose and something special is possible.

So, what do we mean by purpose? This question was explored in some detail at Leadercast 2017 but also previously by John Maxwell the leadership guru. Some of my key takeaways about purpose are as follows:

1. Purpose is across the border from "what's in it for me?"
2. Purpose takes us beyond "me" to "meaning".
3. Purpose is about serving others.
4. When we have a purpose that is bigger than us, we have a calling.

Leadercast 2017 implored us to pay attention to what stirs our hearts and to notice what inspires and ignites us. Maxwell encourages readers and listeners to reflect on what we are passionate about, what energises us, and what we enjoy doing to make a positive difference in any environment.

My purpose has become increasingly clear: "To inspire, guide and serve leaders and teams to unleash potential and be all we can be". My career capital consists of front line military leadership, executive team facilitation, management consulting, performance coaching and project management, sprinkled with entrepreneurship, business administration and book authorship! I know I am energised when I feel part of a leadership team that is daring to believe in truly exceptional performance, and is focused on the right activities and attitude to achieve that goal.

Tim Wigham

Fitness for purpose is an interesting one; firstly, it is important to be well conditioned and prepared to fulfil our purpose, but secondly it is equally important to acknowledge that the suitable solution to an issue is not necessarily the best possible solution but rather the most effective under the prevailing circumstances.

Exceed Performance is currently helping a client team build up their collective fitness and readiness to embark on a drilling campaign in the North Sea. Part of this process is assembling the right skillset, the other part is building the right mindset - one team, one mission, first time right, fit for purpose.

24

PATH TO THE PODIUM

Last weekend I drove seven hours from Aberdeen to Sheffield to join a close friend who I have known for 25 years. We had entered the Masters category of a Paired CrossFit Competition called Inferno Racing. Between Saturday and Sunday, we competed in seven workouts, and at the end of it all, we were fortunate enough to be crowned champions of our age group.

I reflected on the achievement as I drove back up to Aberdeen on Sunday night. It was just another weekend on the calendar but it was a landmark in my life. It was not an amazing athletic achievement by any means, however it was a great reference point for me in terms of perseverance, determination, camaraderie, and the difference between Participation and Podium in any endeavour... I'm referring to the dots that join up to a Podium Performance.

With the benefit of hindsight, there were four differentiators on this occasion:

1. Bootneck Brother - My friend and team mate for this event is not standard issue. He is a Winner on every metric. We joined the Marines together in 1992, and we deployed to the same Unit together the following year. We have worked and trained together in many places including the operational front line. We always have long conversations about all sorts of topics but for the actual competition workouts there was not much need for dialogue; the simple unspoken pact was to go as hard as possible, to work for each other, and to never ever quit. Having this history and congruency turned out to be a significant competitive advantage for an event like this.

2. Competition Capital - Two weeks prior to this event I had competed in an individual competition and was therefore "current" in terms of workouts, expectations, strengths, weaknesses, and most important, strategy. Having been tested recently, I was familiar and confident, I was prepared.

!nspired Too

3. Start Strategy - Ahead of every workout, Dom and I would agree our rep scheme and outline plan. We would then confirm this 5 minutes before GO! Being clear about our collective intent proved massively important when the limbs began to lock. We were ambitious but realistic with our approach and it helped us focus when the competition was close and muscle failure was imminent.
4. Outcome Ownership - Process ownership is critical, it is within our control as athletes and professionals. The right processes will drive the right outcomes. It is for this reason that we reflected on our performance and position as the competition progressed. This helped refine our resolve and rationale for certain strategies, particularly in the Final.

The Final itself was a true test, more of willpower and self-belief than anything else. I felt exhausted going into it and had some concerns about niggling injuries and certain movements, however, it came down to trust in our collective refusal to fail so close to the Finish. We left it all out on the floor and as we crashed over the line at the end of the workout, I was overcome with relief and respect. There was a true sense of satisfaction in finally getting a win after years of training and varying competition results.

We achieved high performance as a Pair on this occasion. Key Podium reference points for me were as follows:

a) Being in a team which feels like family, there is extra commitment to the cause.
b) Joining a proven winner has a winning effect.

c) Being fit and in form is essential.

d) Planning ahead and checking understanding immediately prior to a task is critical.

e) Reviewing and reflecting on each past performance helps to truly own the next.

As a performance guide, I focus on people and process: it is nice to have a recent personal reference point which reinforces the fundamentals of campaign success.

25

LESSONS FROM A PROVEN ENTREPRENEUR

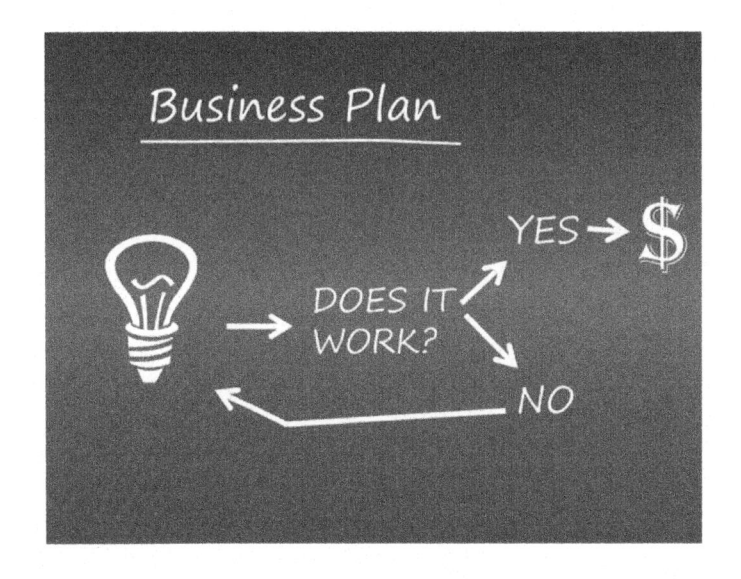

I am fortunate to call some exceptional entrepreneurs my friends. To enhance my own entrepreneurship, I can model their direction and discipline. Dom Moorhouse took

Moorhouse Consulting from singleton to a £20 Million target for successful acquisition in under 5 years. Last week I attended his annual "5YE" Retreat.

Dom's story is nothing short of heroic. He took on the city and the big 5 consultancies and he emerged with a legacy intact... after less than 5 years. What makes him worth listening to is his humility and honesty. I recommend his retreat to any budding entrepreneur because the content is literally a guide to greatness in any field.

The 5 lessons that intrigued and intuitively landed for me were as follows:

1. Strive for professional excellence but don't take yourself too seriously. Have fun while mastering your craft and breaking new ground. This paradox of personal humility and professional will is otherwise described as Level 5 Leadership by Jim Collins after his extensive research into successful organisations. It is proven.

2. Working on the business rather than in the business is crucial for growth. Stepping off the hamster wheel of client delivery is the only way to get a strategic view and to chart a course to the finish line. It starts with a business plan but it needs constant review.

3. Everyone in your business is in sales. Everyone is required and rewarded for the growth of the company. Everyone should be armed with the message and motivation to convert opportunities for new and repeat business. It is the responsibility of all involved to build value for all involved.

4. Accurate and up-to-date Management Information (MI) must be relentlessly and religiously analysed

!nspired Too

and applied. MI is the snap shot that tells the hard truth. It reminds me of the CrossFit Mantra from Greg Glassman "Ignoring your weaknesses is a recipe for incapacity and error"; it is the same for entrepreneurs - gaps in the value proposition and gaps in the value chain need to be addressed immediately. Financial growth can be formulaic; MI provides the insight and the input to the formulae.

5. Business buyers are not necessarily interested in the calibre of the team that built an attractive business, but a high-performance team is needed to succeed, to help codify what the business does, and to build sustainable Intellectual Property (IP) which does interest and attract potential buyers. Without the right people on the bus, the bus will never be built to last or to appeal for acquisition.

Successful entrepreneurs know about performance. I came away from the retreat inspired and ignited to revitalise my enterprise.

26
BEST INDICATORS OF PERFORMANCE CULTURE

People often ask me about the best initial indicators of a team performance culture based on first impression. I always answer that it is about the simple basics. Good or bad, these indicators are typically representative of the overall performance picture.

The first indicator is whether or not members of the organisation are audibly bad-mouthing management or each other. It is amazing how prevalent this is, therefore the absence of negative talk is notable.

The second indicator is whether meetings happen as advertised and on time. Unfortunately, many organisations struggle to start meetings on time and to keep meetings effective. Consistently punctual and valuable meetings are therefore significant.

The third indicator is whether people do what they say they'll do when they say they'll do it. All too often incongruence is the norm; someone promises to get something done but then needs constant reminding. Early delivery on small promises is a massive positive.

Performance Culture of course has much more complexity but these initial indicators have served me well for many years.

27
FIREHOUSE 51

The mindset of first responders is a great reference point for teams seeking high performance. As such, "Chicago Fire" while entertaining, is also intriguingly inspiring. There are some excellent examples of leadership, teamwork, and execution under pressure.

I am always struck by the way the show weaves classic conundrums which are prevalent in most team settings. Leadership decisions need to be made between the "easy way" and the "right way"; the former tends to merely postpone the "tough call". Teamwork is negatively affected by individual agendas which are allowed to evolve unhealthily. Execution for fire fighters is set against a backdrop of high risk, time pressure, and insufficient information - as such, mission command, trust, and superior training is critical.

There are three outstanding leaders depicted in Firehouse 51 but there is also a self-correcting team which will not tolerate "average". The performance culture is that of a close-knit family and their depicted reputation is legendary across Chicago.

The series is not real but the leadership, teamwork, and performance lessons are incredibly relevant to the high risk, high reliability, extraction based industries in which I work as a performance guide.

Firefighters in general are some of the bravest, most selfless heroes around. I am grateful to all of them for their service and sacrifice. I'm also grateful for their mindset which sets the bar for new teams looking to be inspired.

28

STEPPING OFF THE HAMSTER WHEEL

I have had a few recent reminders relating to the excellent analogy of the hamster wheel. There have been times in my life where I felt I was ultra-busy yet going nowhere in terms of genuine, measurable progress. Upon reflection, in most of those cases I stubbornly stepped up the pace rather than

!nspired Too

stepping off to pause and consider why I was doing what I was doing, and how I could be doing it smarter.

With very few exceptions, stepping off has enabled a step change. This is why executive breakaways can be so transformative for a leadership team. The change of scenery and chance to take stock generally inspires a paradigm shift.

At a macro level, I saw this when I took a year away from work to complete my MBA. More recently at a micro level, I saw this when I took 3 days away from a busy work schedule to attend an Entrepreneurs' Retreat.

From a career perspective, I was so passionate about the value of stepping off the hamster wheel, I started two small companies in ten years that ran "breakthrough breakaways" - for professional sports teams in the first instance, and then corporate teams in the second.

Breakaway breakthroughs do not only apply to process and priority, I find there is also a genuine revitalisation of energy borne through the refreshing change of perspective that comes from objective external review.

In summary, retreats and breakaways are a breath of fresh air and if we are on a hamster wheel, we need to get off for two reasons; one - hamster wheels are not healthy for humans, two - the break will allow us to turn the hamster wheel into a helicopter as we build a metaphor more aligned with smart forward progress, elevation, and success.

29
FORGING IDENTITY

Creating a team identity is an exceptionally important early step towards campaign success. Campaign teams usually comprise multiple stake-holders from diverse backgrounds. Individuals and sub teams within the campaign team have their own identities and organisational brands. Unifying everyone involved in a campaign by forging one common identity is vital for collaboration, cohesion, and commitment.

We feel that forging a campaign team identity is so fundamental to accelerated team integration that we have embedded it as one of the initial key steps when guiding a high-performance journey.

Identity is best represented by a unique visual brand or logo. To this end, we work with campaign team members to co-create a truly representative campaign brand of which the whole team can be proud. This brand can then adorn knowledge documents, presentations, posters and even Tee shirts. It is a discreet logo which will only ever be associated with a specific campaign and as such its future appearance can trigger memories and shared reference points for the relevant people, place, and time.

We talk about "one team, one mission" because uniting behind a common cause is so powerful. As Babe Ruth said: "The way a team plays as a whole determines its success. You may have the greatest bunch of individual stars in the world, but if they don't play together, the club won't be worth a dime."

We see this in the world of sport; it is just as prevalent in the world of commerce and industry. Forging, and collectively uniting behind a common identity, makes any campaign team aspiration a lot more possible.

30
LEADING SOCIAL INDICATORS OF A TRUE TEAM

I recently wrote about certain visible behaviours which betray a poor performance culture. This short article will outline some of the subtle behavioural indicators of a true team in any setting; a team much more likely to achieve a high-performance culture based on my observations and experience.

The first element is basic courtesy - this is such a fundamental one. It manifests in various daily interfaces such as greeting colleagues when you see them, and responding to communications in a timely fashion. It needs to be a two-way street; if it feels like one party is constantly having to initiate the courtesy, there is no true team.

The second element is basic trust - this builds on courtesy. A true team has formed and "stormed" to the extent that trust has been earned… It allows for personal growth and for individual expression to benefit the collective. If concerns about trust are regularly voiced, or micro-management is in evidence, there is no true team.

The third element is basic empathy - this builds on courtesy and trust. It means that team members are interested in the challenges of colleagues and that they seek to understand different points of view. If there is no sense that team mates genuinely care or can step into the shoes of others, there is no true team.

The fourth element is basic energy - this is an essential ingredient in any successful team. Energy can be seen and sensed, as can lethargy - an opposite element synonymous with poor performance and disjointed teams… If there is a lack of energy, there is no true team, at least not one that is likely to achieve high performance!

To sum up: in my experience, true teams consist of courteous individuals with high levels of trust, genuine empathy, and high energy. These elements can be detected in a relatively short space of time. Deficiencies in any of these areas will detract from team togetherness and prevent high performance. Get the basic elements in place and build a true team.

31

HOW IMPORTANT ARE REFERENCE POINTS?

Last week I was driving my family from Calgary back to Vancouver in Canada. We decided to stop for a river swim near the highway and spent a pleasant half hour in the water with warm sunshine and wind on our faces. As we were about to leave, we heard the unmistakable growl of a Cougar nearby! With hearts racing we gathered together and quickly agreed a plan to return to the vehicle as safely and efficiently as possible. We made it and did not see the predatory cat, but the kids will never forget the impromptu adrenalin rush.

When I was offshore Ghana on an Oil Rig in 2011, I received the news that my Dad had passed away. I was distraught. When I later found out how he had died, I was devastated. I had to travel overnight back to South Africa and then up to Zimbabwe to confront the situation and help plan the funeral. It was the toughest month of my life.

Since 2010 I have been progressing a PhD research project but have struggled to maintain momentum and up to now have failed to complete the process. It has been a fascinating journey but the end is not yet in sight.

This year several of my medium-term goals were realised; I published my first book, co-secured a number of significant work contracts, and jointly won a masters fitness competition with a valued friend. All three achievements the result of significant "grind" over a number of years.

We all have reference points for family, tragedy, failure and success; these reference points are so important as life throws new challenges and opportunities at us. Nelson Mandela said; "I either win or I learn." If we can tap into key learnings from relevant previous reference points, we can become more and more effective and purposeful. Listing and learning from key reference points can be immensely valuable; give it a go.

32

CROSSING THE RUBICON

A conversation with my business partner Ian recently reminded me of this extraordinary idiom.

"Crossing the Rubicon" means to pass a point of no return, and refers to Julius Caesar's Army crossing the Rubicon River (in the north of Italy) in 49 BC; this was considered an act of insurrection and treason.

In this day and age, when we talk about "crossing the Rubicon", we mean to take a decisive, irrevocable step.

Crossing the Rubicon in a personal or professional sense is basically a game-changer, a paradigm shift, or a step change.

Julius Caesar went on to lead the Roman Empire once he had taken that step.

There is another famous saying: "If you want to take the island, burn the boats!". This inspiring quote also owes its origins to Caesar. The Roman General ordered the burning of his own boats when he saw his officers wavering before taking the coast of Britain.

Fitting that the leader who challenged safe thinking to cross the Rubicon, should defy safe strategy in order to harden the resolve of his men.

In both cases the reward outweighed the risk. It takes courage to break the "rules", failure may result, but fortune tends to favour the brave.

Perhaps it is time to cross the Rubicon...

33

QUOTES TO TAKE YOU ABOVE AND BEYOND

10 quotes which have struck a chord with me over the years...

Tim Wigham

"Out beyond ideas of wrong doing and right doing, there is a field. I'll meet you there." Rumi

"Only a man who knows what it is like to be defeated can reach down to the bottom of his soul and come up with the extra ounce of power it takes to win when the match is even." Mohammed Ali

"Being a hero is not about being unafraid, it is about being scared to death but doing the right thing anyway." Chicago Fire

"The key is not to prioritise what is on your schedule, but to schedule your priorities." Stephen Covey

"Discipline is choosing between what you want now and what you want most." Augusta Kantra

"The scariest moment is always just before you start." Stephen King

"What we see depends mainly on what we look for." Sir John Lubbock

"We cannot solve our problems with the same thinking we used when we created them." Albert Einstein

"Hardships often prepare ordinary people for an extraordinary destiny." C S Lewis

"When you're good at making excuses, its hard to excel at anything else." John Mason

34
DEFINING OUR APPROACH

I often encounter confusion regarding the subtle but distinct differences between coaching, mentoring, consulting and many other people based interventions.

As a performance coach, I have had to clarify first for myself and then for others, the fundamental differences and felt it may be useful to spell out some common definitions with additional emphasis below. These are not perfect, but they provide some food for thought.

Coaching involves skilled and targeted conversations that challenge and support leaders and teams to help themselves, and their business, to excel. The emphasis is on building client confidence, capacity, and internal capability to generate their own solutions to any problem, rather than providing to the client direct solutions to specific problems.

Mentoring guides mentees to find the right direction and to help them develop solutions to career issues. Mentors rely upon having had similar experiences to gain an empathy with the mentee and an understanding of their issues. The emphasis is on the fact that the mentor has specific experience which qualifies him or her to advise these mentees.

Consulting usually involves expert and often experienced professionals in a specific field with wide knowledge of the relevant subject matter. By hiring a consultant, clients have access to deeper levels of expertise than would be financially feasible for them to retain in-house on a long-term basis. The emphasis is on outside solutions to internal problems.

Training is teaching, or developing in oneself or others, any skills and knowledge that relate to specific useful competencies. The emphasis is on developing new competencies that can be assessed and approved in order that the trainee becomes qualified to graduate.

Counselling involves guidance on personal or psychological problems. The emphasis is on listening and talking therapy to helping an individual overcome personal issues.

With these definitions in mind I often reflect on what we do as performance improvement specialists: To some degree we are consultants because we do provide a solution in the form of a proven model for process improvement, but equally we do coach and it is undoubtedly the campaign team that actually generates the results.

I have certainly found it useful to clarify in my own mind how training, mentoring, and counselling differ from the standard remit for a performance coach. In turn it has aided a few conversations I have had on rig campaigns from time to time.

Onwards and upwards.

35
WHY HAVE A REUNION?

!nspired Too

Last weekend it was my privilege to lead a reunion of men who first met a quarter of a century ago. It was a special gathering for a number of reasons and I reflected on these as my train sped from Devon back to London last Sunday afternoon.

Like many similar groups, our foundational shared experience was commando training - a physical, mental, and emotional rollercoaster over 15 months in the early nineties. Since then we have all gone in different directions and only a few of our number continue to serve.

Every time we re-unite as a band of brothers, there is nonstop banter and a huge amount of fun. This time around there was also an element of compassion as one of our number is unwell and could not make the flight from New Zealand.

In order to generate some enthusiasm and energy for this rendezvous, I had setup a "chat-net" on social media - this proved to be an ice breaker and a game changer for a number of reasons; it was an easy way to connect with the group, it was an easy way to remain informed about the ongoing agenda, and it was exclusive to this group of people with a shared past and a shared sense of humour.

The schedule for the weekend was based on a tried and tested formula with some optional activities which could be switched on or off depending on conditions, communication, and collective interest!

The invite for this reunion had gone out to a number of those who actually led our training but unfortunately none could attend. That said, it was the first time this was the case and to a large degree it made for a more intimate and authentic gathering.

A very valuable suggestion was the inclusion of video messages from those that could not make the event: In the end, we received three of these and they were excellent. The final video message was from our friend in New Zealand - a larger than life character who is battling cancer. This message was inspirational under the circumstances but that is what you would expect from the kind of warrior who earned a bravery medal for aiding victims of the Christchurch earthquake, and who joined the All Black squad as one of their management team.

We actually set up a live video conversation after the video message and this truly helped him feel part of our reunion community. Under the circumstances, this 10-minute dialogue exemplified the significance of a reunion - a true sense of care and belonging.

The two-day gathering genuinely allowed enough time for everyone to catch up with one another while spending time back where it all started for us. Many memories were repeated, but many updates were also shared as we re-established connections and currency. New commitments to more frequent contact and even to potential business collaboration, underscored the extensive value of reunions such as this.

I was reminded of three key principles; pulling any team together is immensely rewarding, easy and effective communication is essential, and flexibility based on diverse interests, ensures that morale and momentum can be maintained.

Five years until our next major reunion but continued opportunities to apply these basic principles in everyday life.

36
PLAYING THE SWEEPER

One of our clients recently used an excellent metaphor to describe our performance coaching service. The comment was that our coaches play a vital "sweeper role".

It immediately resonated for me as I envisaged manual and automated sweepers clearing up after operational traffic to ensure that everything is picked up and nothing is left behind.

A sweeper in soccer and field hockey is a player who is positioned in the defensive backline and is responsible for countering any opposing attackers who may get past the other defenders. A key player to marshal the defensive effort and ensure that nothing gets missed.

As I have mentioned before; most of the operational horse-power on any project, is forward focused to ensure that progress continues to be made. This focus is natural and professional. For this reason, it is inevitable that rigorous learning is somewhat compromised, especially when it is a secondary focus for the team.

Investing in an impartial, objective resource who is 100% accountable for driving the learning process and sweeping up after the team, is the only way to be sure that no stone is left unturned in the collective quest for continuous improvement.

The sweeper comment also reminded me of the All Blacks "sweep the sheds" culture which is all about servant leadership and humility - key character traits of any world class coach.

Every day in a project environment, there are opportunities to capture suggestions but sadly all too often these opportunities are missed. Effort is required to record suggestions in accurate detail; it is a full-time job. Even with paperwork available to crews for shift feedback, information capture seldom realises its full potential without a dedicated scribe.

The sweeper role is a leader role; serve the team by guiding improvement through tireless attention to detail and unrelenting follow up in order to ensure nothing is missed.

Sweep on.

37
HOW DO WE GET THE HORSE TO DRINK?

We are all familiar with this popular analogy: "You can take the horse to water but you can't make it drink". It emphasises the fact that no matter how much you advise

!nspired Too

good practice, it is ultimately up to individuals or teams to actually do the practice.

On our performance improvement projects, we often face resistance to recommended disciplines. Interestingly it is not always the same. On some campaigns, it is initial resistance to conducting a review of each operational phase, on others it is disagreement about the need to go through the plan together as a team. We have seen apprehension about video recording and questions about the value of tracking invisible lost time.

I actually prefer resistance, to apathy. The former at least indicates engagement and curiosity. We often remark that the greatest cynics, when converted become the greatest improvement champions.

But how do we get the proverbial horse to drink? The intuitive answer from our perspective is "lead by example and lead with courage". As Ghandi said: "Be the change that you wish to see in the world". Nothing drives improvement like strong leadership. If team members are inspired by the added value and impact of new disciplines like planning meetings or operational reviews, they will be inclined to at least give these initiatives a try.

The gold medal scenario is that front line supervisors buy into the value of good practice even if it involves additional effort, the opposite of this, which I have seen once or twice, is that good practice has to be mandated by project sponsors because it is not being courageously led at the front line.

True coaching is put to the test where human factors are concerned. All leaders, supervisors, and team members are unique so respect is only earned through authentic contribution and genuine listening in order to understand prevalent culture and in some cases, resistance to change.

I love the challenge of creating the right conditions for the horse to actually want to drink; furthermore, I am happiest when I see the horse encouraging the team to do the same.

38
HOW DO WE LEARN?

One of the more obvious gaps our clients are often looking for us to help fill, is the supply of a resource and a tool to support project learning.

To this end we pride ourselves in continually striving to develop exceptional performance coaches and excellent tools to meet and exceed this need.

The theory illustrated here was initially described as the "Four stages for learning any new skill", and was developed by Noel Burch in the 1970s. It has since been frequently attributed to Maslow although the model does not appear in his major works.

I always prefer simple, and this illustration can be so helpful in explaining how we learn a new skill, but also in explaining the stages of implementing good practice such as a rigorous approach to learning.

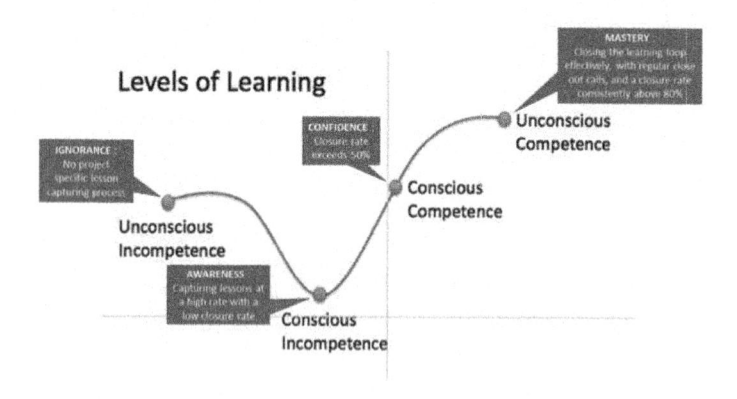

Levels of Learning

- IGNORANCE: No project specific lesson capturing process
- AWARENESS: Capturing lessons at a high rate with a low closure rate
- CONFIDENCE: Closure rate exceeds 50%
- MASTERY: Closing the learning loop effectively, with regular close out rates, and a closure rate consistently above 80%

Unconscious Incompetence → Conscious Incompetence → Conscious Competence → Unconscious Competence

The short trip from Ignorance down into the "valley" of Awareness (otherwise known as the pit of learning) can be a painful one, and the long journey out can seem overwhelming. However, with perseverance and team commitment to the disciplines of lesson capture and closure, the milestone of Confidence can be passed en-route to the summit (and habit) of Mastery!

As Aristotle once said: "We are what we repeatedly do. Excellence, then, is not an act, but a habit."

Our aim is to help enrol the team and accelerate the learning curve which in turn builds a masterful team; one which resists complacency, achieves objectives, promotes safer operations, and delivers ahead of the plan.

When best practice is habitual, our work is done.

39
SHACKLETON LEADERSHIP

There are many articles on Shackleton and his legacy. Like many, I find the stories of his leadership during the failed Endurance voyage to be impossibly inspiring. Words cannot really do justice to the epic magnitude of his conquest over the severest adversity.

Inspired Too

Three key reference points stand out for me when considering Shackleton:

1. His newspaper advertisement to find crew for the Trans-Antarctic Endurance expedition.

MEN WANTED

For hazardous journey, small wages, bitter cold,
long months of complete darkness, constant danger.
Safe return doubtful, honour and
recognition in event of success.

Ernest Shackleton

He had no shortage of applicants.

2. The fact that he was buried in South Georgia years after his incredible previous journey to the island as part of a rescue effort which still astounds explorers to this day. His sheer will power and determination to get help for his stranded men was the very embodiment of "mind over matter".

A fitting resting place for this genuine hero.

3. Shackleton's personal quotes:

"Through endurance we conquer." - Ernest Shackleton

"When I look back at those days I have no doubt that Providence guided us, not only across those

> snowfields, but across the storm-white sea that separated Elephant Island from our landing-place on South Georgia. I know that during that long and racking march of thirty-six hours over the unnamed mountains and glaciers of South Georgia it seemed to me often that we were four, not three. I said nothing to my companions on the point, but afterwards Worsley said to me, 'Boss, I had a curious feeling on the march that there was another person with us.' Crean confessed to the same idea. One feels 'the dearth of human words, the roughness of mortal speech' in trying to describe things intangible, but a record of our journeys would be incomplete without a reference to a subject very near to our hearts." - Ernest Shackleton

In summary, it is well worth reading more about this famous explorer. There are so many leadership lessons to be learned. He was associated with perceived failure but subsequently also, incredible success.

When asked about the heroic age of Antarctic exploration, Sir Raymond Priestley, a contemporary of the explorers of that time gave the following famous comparison:

"Scott for scientific method, Amundsen for speed and efficiency but when disaster strikes and all hope is gone, get down on your knees and pray for Shackleton."

If grace under pressure is a leadership trait, surely Shackleton set the standard.

40
BEATING PROCRASTINATION

Like many, I have struggled with procrastination over the years. I have good intentions, set goals, but then get distracted and delayed... sound familiar?

Recently I had something of an epiphany while listening to "ET" (Eric Thomas) the motivational speaker. What he said is a simple truth but one which has helped me reframe the concept of procrastination.

ET mentions a woman who attended one of his seminars in Australia; she claimed to have a major problem with punctuality and procrastination so he gave her this scenario... "If I offered you a million dollars to meet me at a certain location at 5am, what would you do?" she answered, "I'd be there at 04:59 no matter what!"

ET went on to confirm what we all intuitively know which is that if something is important enough, we will prioritise it and we will be on time. What each of us considers important may differ from one person to the next, but the principle remains the same.

Beating procrastination is about personal priority, reality, and honesty:
1. What is non-negotiable for you?
2. What is genuinely important to you?
3. What do you genuinely value?

ET is known for popularising the quote: "When you want to succeed as bad as you want to breathe, then you'll be successful."

It gets the point across; you have to want something really badly in order to beat procrastination. This is why it is often people like ET who come from nothing and go on to achieve success - there was no fall-back option, getting things done is non-negotiable.

If something is not important enough, it will be sacrificed or put off until another time. To avoid procrastination, we should set goals which align to what we genuinely believe we have to achieve in order to survive and thrive. Then we need to be proactive, and we need to anticipate in order to stay ahead of deadlines and deliverables.

Now lets take a deep breath, and give ourselves a fighting chance.

41
INSPIRING POEMS

I am currently reading a book called "The If Man" by Chris Ash. It is about Leander Starr Jameson, the man whose life inspired Rudyard Kipling to actually write the well-known poem - "IF".

!nspired Too

This has long been my favourite poem because it resonates with my background, my values and my aspirations. As a British South African who grew up in Zimbabwe, I find the pioneers of the Rhodes and Jameson era to be incredibly inspiring in terms of their "can-do" mindset and extraordinary courage in the face of significant adversity.

Jameson epitomised the spirit of discovery, he exemplified mission command and situational leadership time and time again. Most of all, he believed in possible rather than impossible.

Quite simply, he inspired the writing of these words by one of the best poets ever to have put pen to paper. Jameson was clearly a unique individual.

> If you can keep your head when all about you
> Are losing theirs and blaming it on you,
> If you can trust yourself when all men doubt you,
> But make allowance for their doubting too.
> If you can wait and not be tired by waiting,
> Or being lied about, don't deal in lies,
> Or being hated, don't give way to hating,
> And yet don't look too good, nor talk too wise:

> If you can dream—and not make dreams your master;
> If you can think—and not make thoughts your aim;
> If you can meet with Triumph and Disaster,
> And treat those two impostors just the same;
> If you can bear to hear the truth you've spoken
> Twisted by knaves to make a trap for fools,
> Or watch the things you gave your life to, broken,
> And stoop and build 'em up with worn-out tools:

> If you can make a heap of all your winnings
> And risk it on one turn of pitch-and-toss,
> And lose, and start again at your beginnings
> And never breathe a word about your loss;
> If you can force your heart and nerve and sinew
> To serve your turn long after they are gone,
> And so hold on when there is nothing in you
> Except the Will which says to them: "Hold on!"
>
> If you can talk with crowds and keep your virtue,
> Or walk with Kings—nor lose the common touch,
> If neither foes nor loving friends can hurt you,
> If all men count with you, but none too much;
> If you can fill the unforgiving minute
> With sixty seconds' worth of distance run,
> Yours is the Earth and everything that's in it,
> And—which is more—you'll be a Man, my son!
>
> Rudyard Kipling, 1895

If a poem was written about each of our lives, what would it say?

I am reminded that is never too late to create the future and to fill the unforgiving minute with sixty seconds' worth of distance run. Thanks Kipling, and Jameson!

42

THE VALUE OF MIND MAPPING

Reviewing work done to capture learnings and get better is generally accepted as good practice. The challenge can be the motivation of stake holders such that they feel that time spent in a review is beneficial, logical, and most important, that the output is valuable.

To this end, facilitator preparation is key, and a useful tool in this process is the mind map. Simple is generally best, so a logical mind map that helps a participant visualise the work process, and that indicates where lessons have already been learned, is welcome!

We have found that for triggering accurate memory, the mind map is an excellent tool for front line operators. It is easily manipulated on screen and/or easily printed on a sheet of A4.

A lack of preparedness for After Action Reviews is a great way to disillusion the team. Preparation and organisation shows respect and sets the scene for excellence and focus. Be mindful of this and map out the operation to be discussed.

43
DISRUPTING INERTIA

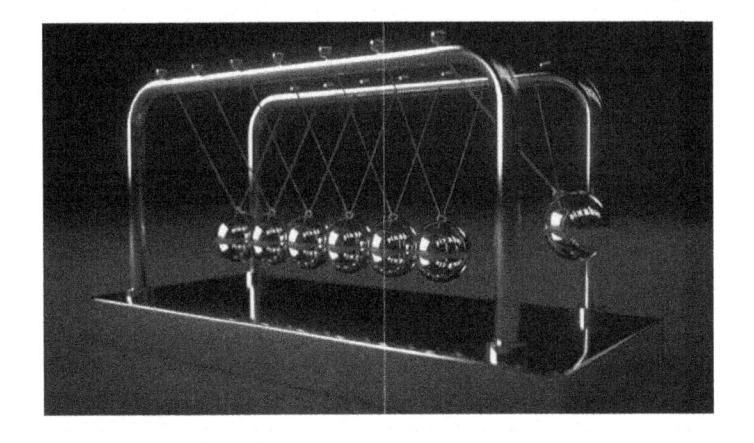

Inertia is the tendency of an object to stay at rest or preserve its state of motion. It could also be described as resistance to change.

Disruption in business terms means to change the traditional way that an industry operates, especially in a new and effective way.

So disrupting inertia is about overcoming resistance to change and creating some positive momentum towards improvement.

We also talk about disrupting team inertia and accelerating the natural learning curve on high-cost, high-profile projects. Acceleration is described as a change in speed, a change in direction, or a change in both.

I was reminded of this perspective while facilitating a planning workshop for an oil company in Aberdeen last week. The session was focused on decommissioning and the assembled team was ready to disrupt inertia by rigorously reviewing the way things were done on the first well abandonment of the campaign.

Dedicated front-line performance coaches had helped the team to capture every lesson from every phase so we were very clear on exactly what had taken place. Collectively we explored all possible ideas to change the approach and to improve execution.

!nspired Too

The resulting list of ideas from the group work was innovative and extensive. Projected time and cost savings are conservatively estimated at weeks, and millions, over a multi-well abandonment campaign.

Performance coaching disrupts inertia because the team have a resource to sweep up after operations and to capture learnings, and because the right planning sessions then pull together the right people at the right time to discuss the right issues and drive accelerated, positive change.

Disrupting inertia is helped by a nudge in the right direction by a proven force for good.

44

"NOT BROKEN" TO "NEEDS FIXING"

Performance Coaching can be a balancing act.

One of the challenges that needs balancing on most projects, is the balance between performance disciplines that are already established habits adding measurable value, performance disciplines that the coach brings to the table and that need implementing, and then the need for new ideas based on new problems, new technology, or a new culture.

From an end-user perspective, it can be tempting to use the line "we've always done it this way", from a coach perspective it can be tempting to say "you should be doing it this way", from a campaign perspective, it is essential that the team says, "what can be done a different way?"

On a two-well wildcat exploration campaign we supported in 2015, there was strong team commitment to implement the performance process before and during the first well, but it was between the two wells when key players spontaneously decided to spell out the "game-changing" ideas, that we compounded the learning and helped the project save $5,000,000.

As coaches, all we did was create the conditions for vision and innovation, it was the team leaders who ultimately seized the day.

Coaching is about helping teams realise their potential. It is about helping team leaders decide to fix what they realise needs fixing.

Good coaches are good balancers too.

45

THE IMPORTANCE OF CONTINUITY

One of the caveats we place on accelerated learning and campaign improvement, and indeed on the aspiration for coaches to be able to step away from a client-sustainable performance process, is the significance and prioritisation of leadership continuity.

As performance coaches, we've found that on some projects a key element of our value proposition is the fact that we represent the continuity. This is not a unique selling point but it is often highlighted and appreciated by clients when they have suffered from a high turnover of frontline leadership.

Sports teams that undergo wholesale changes to the leadership group tend to struggle whereas teams with leader continuity and long-range succession plans tend to succeed.

In a recent Forbes leadership article, Don Yaeger writes the following: "Over the years I've spent studying team dynamics, I've learned that the single greatest predictor of sustained excellence is continuity at the top. If you are a fan of the New England Patriots, you know that the consistent leadership at the helm of your favourite team has much to do with why you're annually relevant."

He goes on to say: "Yet we rarely allow leaders time to truly establish the culture that will allow their team to win... The truth is, building a team and creating a culture takes time and patience."

The All Blacks are surely another great example of leadership continuity, and reassuringly enough, their results are second to none.

Continuity, as a contributing factor to high-performance, cannot be underplayed. It is a critical-success-factor and should be treated as such.

46
LEST WE FORGET

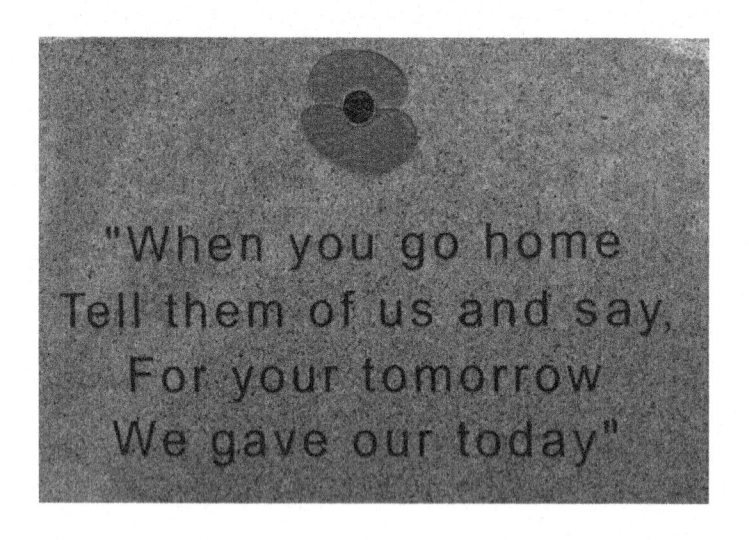

> "When you go home
> Tell them of us and say,
> For your tomorrow
> We gave our today"

15 years ago I visited the Tyne Cot Commonwealth War Graves Cemetery in West Flanders, Belgium with my Father. Like millions of others over the decades, I wandered through the expansive First World War Memorial with a deepening sense of sadness and loss. Most of all, I was finally awakened

and enlightened to a fraction of the scale of the sacrifice made by the men and women who fought for freedom many generations before.

I was struck by the youth of many of those who were killed; many under 20 years old. I was of course also struck by the number of unidentified grave stones which state simply "Known unto God".

When I was still serving in the Royal Marines, I visited the Vietnam War Memorial in Washington DC. Near to the Vietnam Veterans Memorial Wall, I came across a small shop selling prints, one of the prints stopped me in my tracks. It was called "Reflections" and although I couldn't secure my own copy then, I was determined to have one. Several years later I managed to purchase a copy online and I got it shipped to South Africa where I was living at the time.

The print still arrests me as a poignant depiction of war-remembrance and reflection.

This weekend on Armistice Day at the 11th hour of the 11th day of the 11th month, as we tuned in to television coverage from the London Cenotaph and respected the 2-minute silence to remember those who have paid the ultimate price in defence of freedom around the globe, I tried to explain the occasion to my young son. I realised I had a tear in my eye and a lump in my throat so I simply held his hand and stood in silence along with thousands around the UK.

Television coverage of Remembrance Sunday is excellent in my opinion and the poppy is as strong a symbol of remembrance as it has ever been. This well-known poem sums up the tragedy of the battlefields of Western Europe 100 years ago.

Tim Wigham

> In Flanders fields, the poppies blow
> Between the crosses, row on row,
> That mark our place; and in the sky
> The larks, still bravely singing, fly
> Scarce heard amid the guns below.
>
> We are the Dead. Short days ago
> We lived, felt dawn, saw sunset glow,
> Loved and were loved, and now we lie
> In Flanders fields.
>
> Take up our quarrel with the foe:
> To you from failing hands we throw
> The torch; be yours to hold it high.
> If ye break faith with us who die
> We shall not sleep, though poppies grow
> In Flanders fields.
>
> John McCrae, 1915

I hope we never forget what these young heroes sacrificed for our freedom, and as we carry the torch into the new millennium, may we fiercely protect that freedom so that the glorious dead can sleep in peace.

47

LINK IT ALL TOGETHER

Something I have learned is that life is busy! Making progress towards important goals is difficult because we have so many demands placed on such precious little time.

For this reason, the best way I have found to maintain continued momentum on professional aspirations and personal growth, is to link priority goals together.

In my case, LinkedIn (publishing) has provided a central connection for 4 key-chains:
1. Thought leadership about performance-coaching and the value it can add to visionary organisations.
2. Meaningful articles for a series of books focused on frontline performance insights.
3. Research and analysis for a thesis regarding the impact of deliberate performance improvement initiatives on the upstream oil and gas industry.
4. Personal expression through a passion for both writing, and accelerated team learning.

At the centre of the central connection is my profile or my "person". For congruency, credibility, and a degree of authority, I humbly strive for continuous personal growth, and to be able to walk-the-talk in the form of ongoing, value-adding business delivery.

Being "LinkedIn" has literally and figuratively been instrumental for priority-progress and business development in the last few years.

My learning and my recommendation to busy and visionary professionals, is to link goals together where possible. The stronger the link, the stronger the likelihood that one of our key goals will not get left behind.

48
WHAT IS YOUR SENTENCE?

Leadercast includes some fascinating speakers. One of them touched on the concept of focus: "Don't try and be all things to all people, and don't try to do too many things." This is not novel advice or a new idea, but the way the message was put across was thought provoking.

The speaker asked, "What is your sentence?" "What did you do? If people were asked about your impact on the world, what would they say?" There were a few interesting high-profile examples given.

Abraham Lincoln: "He preserved the Union and freed the slaves."

Franklin Roosevelt: "He lifted us out of the great depression and helped us win the war."

We talk about finding our purpose, and to a degree this is a way to begin with the end in mind: If you work out your sentence, you clarify your purpose.

Daniel H Pink recently challenged people to come up with a "what's your sentence?" video. This proved a popular initiative and below are a few examples of some of the more inspiring entries:

"He taught the things that mattered tomorrow, not yesterday or today."

"She helped make the world safer for children through creativity and community, knowing that when the children are safe, so are the grown-ups."

I spent a few minutes thinking about my sentence and came up with this:

"He believed we are all capable of so much more, and he never stopped trying to inspire himself and others, to prove exactly that!"

What is your sentence?

49
CHALLENGER TO CHAMPION

I have been enjoying Don Miller's book about "Building a Story-Brand" over the last few weeks. His "SB7 brand-script" framework is easy to understand and apply. He also repeatedly emphasises the importance of simplicity and clarity. "If you confuse, you'll lose!"

I have taken his lessons about story and applied them to my message about the problems we help our clients to solve.

1. ***If you are a project leader in a heavy industry and are facing a new challenge with a new team, and if you want to do everything possible to get operations right first time, every time, we can help you succeed.***
2. *If you are anxious about achieving objectives under budget, anxious about integrating a team at short notice, anxious about slow learning, or concerned about your reputation, we can help.*
3. We believe every leader and every team wants to learn, and is capable of continually improving to achieve high-performance.
4. At Exceed, we have been privileged to support 30 oil-and-gas drilling / abandonment campaigns over the last 10 years, and we are proud of our contribution to their collective achievements and significant savings.
5. ***Through client feedback and extensive experience, we have developed a structured approach to performance improvement, and a formula for accelerated team learning. We also now have a wealth of relevant and valuable knowledge.***
6. Without exception, the completed campaigns we have supported have safely achieved all objectives, significantly under budget, and with a high agreed-value of implemented team-learnings. The investment in our performance solution pays for itself many times over.
7. But, don't take our word for it, ask our current clients. I can pass on their contact details.

!nspired Too

The journey from challenger to champion involves commitment and consistency, the first step takes courage, the remaining steps enable the transformation to excellence.

Smart challengers seek experienced guidance, smart guides help create champions.

What's your story?

50

VALUE PERCEPTION

I was asked to include a "value proposition" in a recent CTR for a client.

!nspired Too

As I prepared to type it in, I realised that we had some specific feedback this year from two satisfied project sponsors within that particular organisation. I tracked down these testimonials and was reminded that value-perception is our true value-proposition. "Perception is reality" as the saying goes.

This key "end-user" feedback speaks to the "nub" of what we offer:

"The problem we have had is being unable to very rigorously and thoroughly follow our internal learning process with the resources we have, especially offshore where it is most effective.

What Exceed gave us on the recent campaign was the expertise and resources to do this both onshore and more importantly offshore.

Having a dedicated focal point for performance allowed us to review each task in detail in advance. This was done with the crews doing the job, and made sure 1. What we were asking the guys to do was correct, and 2. That it was the best way of doing it.

Exceed guided the capture and documentation of multiple lessons-learned and after-action-review sessions that we "never have the time to capture". They play a great sweeping role."

I ended up simply including the feedback from these two outstanding leaders from within the very same client. It is humbly gratifying to be able to refer to what we have done, versus what we propose to do.

To this client and these sponsors, the value proposed is clearly perceived.

51

REEL TIME

One of our signature team building events at the Cape Leadership Centre in Cape Town was "Reel Time", a fun but relevant team video-production experience which encouraged work groups to get creative, but also, to get

!nspired Too

"real" about challenges at work that needed to be addressed and overcome. The results were always inspiring, and always effective as a vehicle for driving a message home.

A good friend of mine takes snippets of video every day of the year. At the end of each year, he then creates a "highlight-reel" of the year gone past, with one second from each and every day, and subsequently, a 6-minute video as a great reference for the family.

I grew up in Zimbabwe, a beautiful country which has been badly led for decades. Recently there has been cause for celebration and hope, as change has finally swept across the land, signalling a new dawn, new hope, and a new president. The advent of live social media video and short video clips, enabled a real sense of being part of this historic event, particularly footage of thousands in the streets of Harare, hooting, singing, waving, and weeping for joy!

Video is now being used to effectively post updates on social and professional media platforms. It is a way to inform, instruct, and inspire.

For performance management and effective communication, consider getting more "reel" next year.

52
BEST YEAR EVER

Between Christmas and New Year, I downloaded and listened to the audio-book by Jim Rohn called "How to have Your Best Year Ever". It was effectively a presentation he had given back in the 1990s, but interestingly, the principles he covered were completely relevant for 2018.

The key takeaway for me was about backing myself to fulfil my purpose through the pursuit of excellence: Set specific goals and take disciplined action.

In the past I have applied the principles of "Best Year Yet": Ensure the learnings from last year guide the planning for next year, then set specific goals and take disciplined action.

There is a well-known saying by Graeme Edwards: "It's not the plan that is important, it's the planning."

My point is that by taking some time at the beginning and end of each calendar year, to consider the recent past as well as the approaching future, we consciously unpack the sub-conscious to highlight and prescribe critical-happiness-factors for a more fulfilling and productive year.

I know that no plan survives unscathed, however, I also know that no planning limits our ability to influence happiness and fulfilment.

"Best year ever" sounds better to me than "just another year", so I will build on the proven benefits of positive thinking to attract what I hope to achieve.

Equally, I sincerely hope that you take some time to plan for your "best year ever" next year!

"I am an optimist. It does not seem too much use being anything else."
Winston Churchill

About The Author

Tim Wigham grew up in Southern Africa and has dual British and South African citizenship; he served in the British Commandos for 8 years between 1992 and 2000 before completing his Full Time MBA in Cape Town 2001.

Tim then specialized in the facilitation of SME executive leadership breakaways across a range of industries to build strong cohesion, as well as clear strategy, mission, vision and authentic company values.

In the sports industry, Tim worked on mental toughness with several of the Springbok Rugby players who went on to be World Cup Winners in 2007.

Tim is currently the Head of Performance at Exceed in Aberdeen. He has worked as a performance improvement expert in the Energy Sector since 2008.

Tim is based in the North East of Scotland; he is married and has 3 young children. His main interests include writing, reading, travel and "CrossFit". He also enjoys blogging about "Inspiration".